The Psychology of Kindle Sales: How to Sell your eBooks on Amazon KDP:

The Secret and Profitable Ways to Sell More Books

Copyright @ 2023 by **Israel Joshua Chukwubueze**

This book may be purchased in bulk for educational, business, fundraising, or sales promotional use.

ISBN:

Published by: **Ekesy In-Outdoor Company**

10B, Mufutau Opeifa Street, Oke-Odo, Ile-Epo B/Stop, Alimosho, Lagos, Nigeria

Email: ekesygroup@gmail.com

Tel: 08038154459, 08132228534

Printed by: **Demrok Prints**

For information, please contact us @

ekesygroup@gmail.com

israeljoshua.com.ng

Call: 08064342968, 08038154459

WATSAPP: 08132228534

TABLE OF CONTENT

Bonuses

Dedication

To the Almighty God, the source of inspiration and unwavering support, I offer my deepest gratitude. It is with immense reverence that I acknowledge your divine guidance in the creation of this book, **"The Psychology of Kindle Sales: How to Sell Your eBooks on Amazon KDP."**

To My Children:

My greatest joy and inspiration, my children, this book is dedicated to you. You are the driving force behind my relentless pursuit of knowledge and success. I hope that as you grow, you will find within these pages the wisdom and passion to pursue your own dreams and aspirations.

To My Beloved Mother:

My dearest mother, your unwavering love and encouragement have been the cornerstone of my life. Your sacrifices and belief in my potential have paved the way for my endeavors. This dedication is a small token of my immense gratitude for your unending support and love.

To My Readers:

To all the readers who have embarked on this journey with me, I dedicate this book to you. Your curiosity and thirst for knowledge are what drive authors to share their insights and discoveries. Your trust in my words and your commitment to personal growth make it all worthwhile. It is my hope that the knowledge contained within these pages enriches your life and empowers you to reach new heights.

As I penned the words that fill the chapters of this book, it was with each of you in mind. To God, my children, my beloved mother, and my cherished readers, I express my profound appreciation for your unwavering support and belief in my endeavors.

May this book serve as a beacon of knowledge and inspiration, guiding its readers toward a brighter future and greater success on their own paths. With your presence and encouragement, I find the strength to continue my literary journey, and for that, I am eternally grateful.

With heartfelt dedication,

Israel Joshua Chukwubueze

Preface

Once known as Christopher Ekene Okade, I stand today as Israel Joshua Chukwubueze, a testament to the transformative power of identity, resilience, and the unwavering pursuit of a dream. As I embark on this journey to introduce you to "The Psychology of Kindle Sales: How to Sell Your eBooks on Amazon KDP," I wish to share the extraordinary path that led me to this moment.

My journey into the world of writing and publishing began with a profound passion for knowledge and the burning desire to share it. I discovered early in life that the written word possessed a unique magic, capable of bridging the gap between worlds, connecting people across time and space, and transcending barriers of culture and circumstance.

The transformation from Christopher Ekene Okade to Israel Joshua Chukwubueze is more than a change of name; it represents a personal evolution that mirrors the transformation of my dreams. It was during this transition that I found the courage to pursue my true passion: writing and sharing knowledge. With a new name came a renewed sense of purpose, an unwavering commitment to the art of the written word, and a dedication to helping others achieve their own literary aspirations.

"The Psychology of Kindle Sales" is the culmination of my personal and professional journey. It is a testament to the transformative power of embracing one's true self and following one's deepest passions. I believe that every one of us has a unique purpose, a calling that, when heeded, can ignite the flames of inspiration in others.

In this book, you will find a comprehensive guide to navigating the complex world of eBook sales on Amazon Kindle Direct Publishing. It's not just about sharing my knowledge; it's about empowering you to unleash your potential as an author, to reach your audience, and to fulfill your dreams.

The journey of writing this book has been marked by countless hours of research, trial and error, and the relentless pursuit of excellence. I've delved into the intricacies of eBook promotion, the art of crafting bestsellers, the power of metadata optimization, and the strategic nuances of multi-platform publishing. It is my hope that the wisdom and insights contained within these pages will serve as a guiding light on your path to eBook success.

As you delve into "The Psychology of Kindle Sales," I invite you to not only learn from my experiences but also to draw inspiration from my personal journey. Embrace your true identity, harness your passions, and embark on your own transformative journey.

May this book be the spark that ignites your literary aspirations, propels your eBooks to new heights, and connects you with readers around the world. Your journey as an author begins here.

With unwavering dedication to the power of the

written word,

Israel Joshua Chukwubueze

Introduction

The world of self-publishing has seen an incredible revolution in recent years, with Amazon Kindle being at the forefront of this digital publishing transformation. Kindle Direct Publishing (KDP) has empowered authors to publish their books independently and make them available to millions of readers worldwide. However, with the increasing number of authors self-publishing their books on Amazon Kindle, it has become increasingly challenging to stand out and make a name for yourself in this crowded marketplace.

If you're an aspiring author, you may have already published your book on Amazon Kindle, but you're struggling to get the sales and reviews you need to make it successful. You may be asking yourself, "What am I doing wrong? Why am I not selling on Amazon?" These are questions that many authors have asked themselves at some point in their self-publishing journey.

The good news is that there are practical and proven strategies that you can implement to increase your book's visibility, get more sales and reviews, and ultimately achieve success on Amazon Kindle. This book is designed to guide you through these strategies and help you unleash the power of Amazon Kindle to sell your first 1000 copies, get reviews without breaking a sweat, and earn $1,000 to $20,000 per month.

In this book, you'll learn how to:

- Write a good and trending book that readers will love.
- Choose between free and paid promotions and the benefits of each.
- Optimize your Amazon KDP book's metadata for maximum searchability and sales.
- Use standalone and series books to your advantage.
- Build an email list and leverage its importance.
- Use giveaways to your advantage.
- Get your first 1000 sales and up to 50 reviews.
- Ask for reviews effectively.
- Develop pricing strategies that work.
- Promote your other books within your book.
- Link your Amazon Author page within your book.
- Find a profitable niche for your Kindle book.
- Conduct keyword research to optimize your book for search.
- Avoid things that can hurt your book's ranking.
- Use your own website to your advantage.
- Use social media platforms and YouTube videos to promote your book.
- Sell on other platforms and increase your reach.

Each chapter in this book is designed to provide practical advice, tips, and strategies that you can apply immediately to increase your book's visibility and sales on Amazon Kindle. With this book as your guide, you'll be able to take your self-publishing journey to the next level and achieve the success you deserve.

Finally, as a bonus, we'll also show you how to use ChatGPT to speed up your book upload and promotion process. With this valuable tool at your disposal, you'll be able to streamline your publishing journey and achieve success faster than ever before.

So, let's dive in and unleash the power of Amazon Kindle!

About the Author:
Israel Joshua Chukwubueze

The Author's Official Website
Learn more about the Author's Passion, Talents, and Skills

Click here to Learn more...

I know you will Enjoy this Book and don't forget to leave a review for this book.
Click Here to Leave a Review!

Click here to **Download Bonus Workbook PDF** Format

Chapter 1: Why you are not selling on Amazon

If you are an independent author trying to sell your book on Amazon, you may be struggling to get your book seen by potential buyers. You may have spent hours crafting the perfect book title, designing an eye-catching cover, and selecting the right categories and keywords for your book. However, despite your best efforts, your book may not be selling as well as you had hoped.

The big reason you are not selling on Amazon is that nobody is seeing your book. In other words, your book is not getting enough visibility or exposure. There are millions of books available on Amazon, and it can be challenging to stand out from the crowd.

Fortunately, there are a few advertising options that you can use to increase your book's visibility on Amazon and drive more sales. These options include using free promotional ads, free promotional countdown ads, or paid ads.

- **Use Free Promotional Ads**

One of the most popular advertising options for independent authors on Amazon is the free promotional ad. This advertising option allows you to offer your book for free for a limited time, usually between one and five days.

During this promotional period, your book will be listed in the free books section on Amazon, which can increase your book's visibility to potential buyers. Many readers browse the free books section on Amazon regularly, and offering your book for free can attract new readers and help you build a fan base.

However, it is essential to note that offering your book for free does not guarantee that readers will leave reviews or purchase your other books. To make the most of your free promotional ad, you should include a call-to-action in your book's description, encouraging readers to leave reviews or sign up for your mailing list.

- **Use Free Promotional Countdown Ads**
Another option for advertising your book on Amazon is the free promotional countdown ad. This advertising option allows you to offer your book for a discounted price for a limited time, usually between one and seven days.

During the promotional period, your book will be listed in the discounted books section on Amazon, which can increase your book's visibility to potential buyers. Offering your book for a discounted price can be an effective way to attract readers who are looking for a deal.

Similar to the free promotional ad, you should include a call-to-action in your book's description, encouraging readers to leave reviews or sign up for your mailing list. You can also use the promotional countdown ad to promote your other books or upcoming releases.

- **Use Paid Ads**

If you have a budget for advertising, you may want to consider using paid ads to promote your book on Amazon. Amazon offers several advertising options, including sponsored product ads, sponsored brand ads, and product display ads.

Sponsored product ads allow you to promote your book in the search results and product dctail pages, while sponsored brand ads allow you to promote your brand and multiple products in the search results. Product display ads allow you to promote your book on related product detail pages or in customer review sections.

Paid ads can be an effective way to increase your book's visibility and attract potential buyers. However, it is essential to monitor your ad performance carefully and adjust your ad targeting and budget accordingly.

In conclusion, if you are struggling to sell your book on Amazon, it may be because nobody is seeing your book. Using free promotional ads, free promotional countdown ads, or paid ads can increase your book's visibility and attract potential buyers. However, it is essential to include a call-to-action in your book's description, encouraging readers to leave reviews or sign up for your mailing list. With the right advertising strategy, you can increase your book sales and grow your fan base on Amazon.

Chapter 2: Free verse Paid Promotion

Use Free and Paid Books to Increase Sales

As a self-published author on Amazon KDP, it can be challenging to increase sales and gain visibility for your books. One effective strategy is to use both free and paid books to promote your work and increase sales.

Using Free Books to Drive Sales to Paid Books:

Offering a free book can be an excellent way to promote your brand and reach a wider audience. When readers download your free book, you have the opportunity to capture their email address and build your email list. You can use your email list to promote your paid books, which can drive sales and increase your visibility on Amazon.

Here are some tips for using free books to drive sales to your paid books:

1. **Choose the right book to offer for free.** Consider offering the first book in a series or a book that complements your paid books. You want to provide value to your readers and entice them to purchase your other books.

2. **Promote your free book.** Use social media, book promotion sites, and your email list to

promote your free book. Encourage readers to share your book with their friends and family.

3. **Include a call-to-action in your free book.** At the end of your free book, include a call-to-action that encourages readers to purchase your other books. Provide a link to your paid books and a brief description of what they can expect.

4. **Use your email list to promote your paid books.** Once you have captured the email address of a reader who has downloaded your free book, you can promote your paid books to them. Use your email list to provide updates on new releases, promotions, and discounts.

Using Paid Books to Increase Sales:
While offering a free book can be an effective way to build your brand and increase visibility, selling books is ultimately how you will generate revenue.

Here are some tips for using paid books to increase sales:

1. **Choose the right price point.** Research the prices of similar books in your genre and set your price point accordingly. Consider offering promotions and discounts to entice readers to purchase your books.

2. **Optimize your book listing.** Use keywords and categories to optimize your book listing and increase your visibility on Amazon. Use a compelling book description and cover design to

entice readers to purchase your book.

3   **Promote your book.** Use social media, book promotion sites, and your email list to promote your book. Consider partnering with influencers and book bloggers to reach a wider audience.

4   **Encourage reviews.** Encourage readers to leave reviews of your book on Amazon. Positive reviews can increase your visibility and credibility on the platform.

In conclusion, using both free and paid books can be an effective strategy for increasing sales on Amazon KDP. By offering a free book, you can capture email addresses and promote your paid books to a wider audience. By optimizing your book listing and promoting your paid books, you can increase visibility and generate revenue.

How best and when to use Amazon `Free Book Deal` promotions for my kindle ebook, and possibly generate emails lists, make some sales, and rank my book on amazon

The Free Book Deal promotion is another promotional tool offered by Amazon that allows you to offer your Kindle ebook for free for a limited time. This can be a powerful way to generate interest in your book, build your email list, make some sales, and potentially improve your book's rank on Amazon.

Here are some tips on how to use the Free Book Deal effectively:

1. **Choose the right time:** As with the Kindle Countdown Deal, timing is crucial when it comes to running a Free Book Deal promotion. Consider scheduling your promotion around a holiday or event related to the theme of your book, or when you expect to have the most traffic on your book's page. You can also coordinate with book promotion sites or newsletters to schedule your promotion at a time when they can help promote it to their subscribers.

2. **Promote your promotion:** Once you've scheduled your Free Book Deal promotion, it's important to get the word out to potential readers. Share the promotion on your website, social media accounts, and other relevant platforms, and consider using paid advertising to reach a wider audience. You can also submit your promotion to relevant book promotion sites and newsletters to get even more exposure. Make sure to include a call-to-action in your promotion, encouraging readers to sign up for your email list or follow you on social media.

3. **Build your email list:** A Free Book Deal promotion can be a great way to build your email list. Offer a free bonus or incentive to readers who sign up for your mailing lists, such as a free chapter of your next book or a discount

on a future purchase. This can help you turn one-time readers into loyal fans who will be more likely to buy your future books.

4   Consider offering a related book: Once readers have downloaded your free book, consider offering a related book or sequel at a discounted price. This can help you capitalize on the interest generated by the Free Book Deal promotion and generate additional sales.

5   **Follow up after the promotion:** After the Free Book Deal promotion is over, don't forget to follow up with readers who downloaded your book. Encourage them to leave reviews, sign up for your mailing list, or follow you on social media to stay up to date on future promotions and book releases.

Overall, a Free Book Deal promotion can be a powerful tool for generating interest in your book, building your email list, and generating sales. By choosing the right time, promoting your promotion, building your email list, and following up with readers, you can turn one-time readers into loyal fans who will be more likely to buy your future books.

Amazon Count-Down Promotion
Amazon Count Down Promotion is a marketing strategy that is used to promote books on Amazon Kindle. It allows authors to discount their books for a specific period of time, usually up to 7 days, and

encourage potential buyers to purchase the book during that time frame. However, if you use the Count Down promotion wrongly, it will not work, and chances are people will not see your promotion.

The big reason you are not selling on Amazon is that nobody is seeing your book. While book title, book cover design, or categories and keywords listing do matter, the major reason your book is not selling is that nobody is seeing it. Therefore, you need to advertise your book to get it seen.

To use the Count Down promotion successfully, you need to make sure people are willing to pay for your book. This means that your book should have a great cover, an enticing blurb, and excellent reviews. These factors will make your book stand out and attract potential buyers.

Moreover, it is essential to combine Count Down promotion with Paid Ads. This will increase the visibility of your book and the chances that people will buy it. Paid ads will put your book in front of potential buyers, increasing the chances that they will see it and be tempted to purchase it.

Before running a Count Down promotion, it is crucial to plan ahead. Choose the right timing for your promotion, and make sure it coincides with your target audience's availability. Also, set a realistic goal for your promotion and make sure it is achievable.

During the promotion period, it is essential to promote it on social media platforms and other relevant websites. Use hashtags and keywords to make your promotion stand out, and encourage your followers to share it with their networks.

One important thing to note is that you should not rely solely on Count-Down promotion to sell your book. It is just one marketing strategy among many. Therefore, it is essential to have a comprehensive marketing plan that includes other strategies such as email marketing, social media marketing, and paid ads.

In conclusion, Count Down promotion is an effective marketing strategy that can help increase book sales on Amazon Kindle. However, to make it work, you need to have a great book, combine it with Paid Ads, plan ahead and promote it on social media platforms and relevant websites. Remember, it is just one marketing strategy, and it should be part of a comprehensive marketing plan that includes other strategies to maximize your book's visibility and sales.

how best and when to use Kindle Countdown Deal promotions for my kindle ebook.

The Kindle Countdown Deal is a promotional tool offered by Amazon that allows you to offer your Kindle ebook at a discounted price for a limited time. This can be a powerful way to drive sales and increase visibility for your book, but it's important to use it strategically to get the most out of the promotion. Here are some tips on how to use the Kindle Countdown Deal effectively:

1. **Choose the right time:** Timing is crucial when it comes to running a Kindle Countdown Deal. Consider scheduling your promotion around a holiday or event related to the theme of your book, or when you expect to have the most traffic on your book's page. Also, keep in mind that it's often best to run promotions for shorter periods, like three to seven days, to create a sense of urgency and encourage readers to buy now.

2. **Price your book strategically:** The Kindle Countdown Deal allows you to offer your book at a lower price for a limited time, but you still need to price it strategically to maximize your profits. Experiment with different price points to find the sweet spot that generates the most sales while still giving you a good return on your investment.

3. **Promote your promotion:** Once you've scheduled your promotion and set your price, it's important to get the word out to potential readers. Share the promotion on your website, social media accounts, and other relevant platforms, and consider using paid advertising to reach a wider audience. You can also submit your promotion to relevant book promotion sites

and newsletters to get even more exposure.

4   **Follow up after the promotion:** After the Kindle Countdown Deal is over, don't forget to follow up with readers who bought your book during the promotion. Encourage them to leave reviews, sign up for your mailing list, or follow you on social media to stay up to date on future promotions and book releases.

Overall, the Kindle Countdown Deal can be a powerful promotional tool when used strategically. By choosing the right time, pricing your book strategically, promoting your promotion, and following up with readers, you can generate sales and build a loyal reader base for your Kindle ebook.

Chapter 3: Write Good and Trending Book

The best way to sell more books is to write good books with compelling Titles and also to write books on trending topics

Writing a good book is key to succeeding as a self-published author on Amazon KDP. However, in addition to writing a good book, it's important to also consider what topics are currently trending and likely to be in high demand by readers.

Here are some tips for writing a good, needed, and trending book on Amazon KDP:

1. **Choose a compelling topic:** When choosing a topic for your book, consider what topics are currently trending and in high demand. Look at bestseller lists, book blogs, and social media to get a sense of what readers are interested in. You can also consider writing about a topic that you are passionate about or have expertise in.

2. **Research your topic:** Once you've chosen a topic, it's important to research it thoroughly. This can help you identify any gaps in the market that your book can fill, as well as ensure that your book is accurate and up-to-date. Use credible sources such as academic journals, industry reports, and news articles to gather

information.

3   **Write a compelling title:** Your book title is
    the first thing readers will see, so it's important
    to make it compelling and memorable. Consider
    using keywords related to your topic, as well as
    descriptive and attention-grabbing language.

4   **Write in a clear and engaging style:** When
    writing your book, it's important to write in a
    clear and engaging style that will keep readers
    interested. Avoid jargon and overly technical
    language, and consider using storytelling
    techniques to make your book more engaging.

5   **Use visuals and multimedia:** Adding visuals
    and multimedia to your book can help make it
    more engaging and interesting to readers.
    Consider using charts, graphs, images, and
    videos to illustrate your points and break up the
    text.

6   **Edit and proofread your book:** Once you've
    written your book, it's important to edit and
    proofread it carefully. This can help ensure that
    your book is free of errors and flows smoothly.
    Consider hiring a professional editor or
    proofreader if you're not confident in your own
    editing skills.

By writing a good, needed, and trending book on
Amazon KDP, you can increase your chances of
success as a self-published author. By choosing a

compelling topic, researching it thoroughly, writing in a clear and engaging style, using visuals and multimedia, and editing and proofreading carefully, you can create a book that readers will love and recommend to others.

Chapter 4: Numbers is the Game

Another Reason you are not selling is that you don't an enough books

When it comes to selling books on Amazon, one of the key factors that can significantly impact your success is the number of books you have published. If you only have a few books available, your sales will likely be limited. On the other hand, if you have a large number of books published, your chances of making consistent sales increase significantly.

Here are some reasons why having a large number of books can benefit your sales on Amazon:

1   **More books increase your visibility:** When you have more books published, you have a better chance of getting noticed by potential readers. Amazon's algorithms are designed to show readers books that are relevant to their interests and search history. The more books you have published, the more chances you have to show up in search results and recommendation lists.

2   **More books increase your credibility:** Having a large number of published books can also increase your credibility as an author. When readers see that you have a large catalog of

books available, they may be more likely to trust you as an author and consider purchasing your books.

3   **More books increase your earning potential:** The more books you have published, the more potential you have for earning money. While not every book will be a bestseller, having a large number of books available for purchase means that you have more opportunities to generate sales and income.

However, it's important to note that not all books will perform equally well. Some books may generate a lot of sales, while others may not sell at all. Therefore, it's important to continue creating and publishing more books in order to increase your chances of success.

If you're new to publishing on Amazon, it can be daunting to think about publishing hundreds of books.

But there are strategies you can use to publish more books without sacrificing quality. Here are some tips:

- **Plan your writing schedule:** Set aside dedicated time to write and stick to it. You don't have to write an entire book in one sitting, but committing to a regular writing schedule can help you produce more content over time.

- **Repurpose your content:** Look for ways to repurpose content you've already created. For example, you could turn a blog post series into a book or expand on a popular topic you've already covered in a previous book.

- **Use ChatGPT to write more book:** ChatGPT is a Game Changer, you can use ChatGPT to create your book, starting from coming up with the book idea, generating the book title, chapters, cover design idea, keywords, category, the book description, etc

- **Outsource some tasks:** If you're struggling to keep up with the demands of publishing, consider outsourcing some tasks. For example, you could hire an editor or cover designer to help you produce more high-quality books.

Having a large number of books available for sale on Amazon can significantly increase your chances of success as an author. While it may take time to build up a large catalog of books, it's important to keep creating and publishing content in order to reach your full potential as an author.

To Write more Books Effortless. I recommended my book for you: **How To Use ChatGPT to Write a Book Within 24 Hours.**
Check for the link within the book and click on it to Order one.

Type of books to watch for and publish on Amazon:

1   **Bestsellers:** Books that have already proven to be popular with readers, whether in a particular genre or across a range of genres. These books often have a large existing audience that is eager to buy more from the author.

2   **Trending Topics:** Books that cover current trends or hot topics that people are talking about. These books can be in a variety of genres, from current events and politics to popular culture and entertainment.

3   **Self-Help:** Books that provide guidance or advice to readers on how to improve their lives, overcome challenges, or achieve their goals. These books can cover a wide range of topics, from relationships and personal growth to business and finance.

4   **How-To Guides:** Books that teach readers how to do something, whether it's cooking, DIY projects, or computer programming. These books can be both informative and entertaining and can appeal to a wide range of audiences.

5   **Seasonal Books:** Books that tie in with holidays, special events, or particular times of the year. For example, cookbooks with recipes for Christmas or Halloween, or children's books about back-to-school or summer vacation.

6   **Niche Genres:** Books that cater to specific audiences or interests, such as sci-fi, fantasy,

romance, or mystery. These books can be successful if they are well-written and have a dedicated audience that is willing to buy.

7 **Memoirs and Autobiographies:** People love reading about the lives of others, especially famous people. Memoirs and autobiographies can be successful on Amazon, particularly if they cover a subject that is of interest to readers. For example, books about successful business people, musicians, or athletes can be popular.

8 **Children's Books:** Parents are always on the lookout for new books to read to their children, and children's books can be a lucrative market on Amazon. Successful children's books often have strong illustrations and engaging stories that capture the attention of young readers.

9 **Historical Fiction:** Historical fiction can be a popular genre on Amazon, particularly if the author is able to weave together a compelling story set in a well-researched historical context. Popular historical fiction books often transport readers to another time and place and provide a glimpse into a bygone era.

10 **Thrillers and Suspense:** Thrillers and suspense novels can be popular on Amazon, particularly if they are fast-paced and keep readers on the edge of their seats. Successful thrillers often have strong plots, complex characters, and unexpected twists and turns that

keep readers guessing.

11 **Romance:** Romance novels can be a lucrative genre on Amazon, particularly if the author is able to create compelling characters and a strong emotional connection between them. Successful romance novels often have well-developed plots and settings that allow readers to escape into a world of love and passion.

12 **Fantasy:** Fantasy novels can be popular on Amazon, particularly if they create a fully-realized world with its own unique rules and systems. Successful fantasy novels often have compelling characters and intricate plots that keep readers engaged from beginning to end.

13 **Science Fiction:** Science fiction can be a popular genre on Amazon, particularly if it deals with current or futuristic technologies and ideas. Successful science fiction novels often explore big ideas and concepts, while still telling an engaging story with relatable characters.

14 **Business and Finance:** Business and finance books can be popular on Amazon, particularly if they provide actionable advice to readers on how to improve their financial situations. Successful business and finance books often have well-researched information and practical tips that readers can apply to their own lives.

15 **Health and Wellness:** Health and wellness

books can be popular on Amazon, particularly if they offer readers practical advice on how to improve their physical or mental health. Successful health and wellness books often have well-researched information and actionable tips that readers can apply to their own lives.

Overall, you need to publish lots of books, look at books that you love but most importantly there is a market for it, and also just checkout what other people are selling and getting more reviews; you can also create similar books and please don't hard-copy them, amazon might penalize you for doing so, just create your own version, look at what they are not doing right and well, and do a better version of it, be creative.

Chapter 5: Optimizing Your Amazon KDP Book's Metadata for Maximum Searchability and Sales

As an author or publisher, you want your book to be easily discoverable by readers searching for books in your genre. The Amazon KDP (Kindle Direct Publishing) platform provides you with the tools to optimize your book's metadata to increase its visibility and ultimately drive more sales. In this article, we will walk you through the step-by-step process of setting up your book's metadata for maximum searchability.

Title and Subtitle

The title and subtitle of your book are the first pieces of metadata that potential readers will see. You want to ensure that they accurately reflect the content of your book and use relevant keywords to improve searchability. Here are a few tips to consider:

1.   **Be specific**: Avoid using generic titles that don't accurately describe the content of your book. Instead, use descriptive titles that tell readers what your book is about.

2.   **Include keywords**: Use relevant keywords in your title and subtitle that potential readers might use to search for books in your genre. For example, if you've written a romance novel set in Paris, you might include keywords like "Paris," "romance," and "love"

in your title and subtitle.

3.   **Keep it short**: Your title and subtitle should be concise and easy to remember. Avoid using long or complicated titles that might be difficult for readers to remember.

Book Description

Your book description is the second most important piece of metadata after your title and subtitle. It's a chance to convince potential readers to buy your book by giving them a taste of what they can expect to find inside. Here are some tips to consider:

1.   **Be clear and concise**: Your book description should be short and to the point. Use simple language and avoid using jargon or technical terms that readers might not understand.

2.   **Highlight the benefits**: Explain to readers what they will gain from reading your book. What problems will it help them solve? What questions will it answer? What entertainment value will it provide?

3.   **Include keywords**: Use relevant keywords in your book description to improve searchability. Again, think about the terms potential readers might use to search for books in your genre and include those keywords in your description.

4.   **Include a call to action**: End your book

description with a clear call to action that encourages readers to buy your book. For example, you might say something like, "If you're looking for an exciting new romance set in the city of love, buy my book today!"

5. **Amazon will not accept any of the following information in the description:**

- Pornographic, obscene, or offensive content
- Phone numbers, physical mail addresses, email addresses, or website URLs
- Reviews, quotes, or testimonials
- Requests for customer reviews
- Advertisements, watermarks on images or videos, or promotional material
- Time-sensitive information (for example, dates of promotional tours, seminars, or lectures)
- Availability, price, alternative ordering information (for example, links to other websites for placing orders)
- Spoiler information for Books, Music, Video, or DVD (BMVD) listings
- Any keywords or book tags phrases

Categories and Keywords

Your book's categories and keywords are critical to improving its discoverability on Amazon. They help readers find your book when they search for books in your genre. Here's how to set them up:

1. **Choose the right categories**: Select the two categories that best describe your book. Amazon provides a list of categories to choose from, so make sure you select the ones that are most relevant to your book.

2. **Choose relevant keywords**: Select up to seven keywords that accurately describe your book. Again, think about the terms potential readers might use to search for books in your genre and include those keywords.

3. **Avoid keyword stuffing**: Don't try to cram as many keywords as possible into your book's metadata. This is known as keyword stuffing and can hurt your book's discoverability.

Author Bio and Editorial Reviews

Your author bio and editorial reviews are additional pieces of metadata that can help convince potential readers to buy your book. Here's how to set them up:

1. **Write a compelling author bio**: Your author bio should be short and to the point. Highlight your relevant experience and credentials, and make sure to include a call to action that encourages readers to buy your book.

2. **Include editorial reviews: Editorial reviews are endorsements from respected publications or industry experts. If you have received any such reviews, make sure to include them in your

book's metadata.

3   **Use social proof**: If your book has received positive reviews from readers on Amazon or Goodreads, include a quote from one of these reviews in your book description or author bio. This can help build social proof and convince potential readers to buy your book.

Book Cover

Your book's cover is the first thing readers will see when they come across your book on Amazon. It's important to ensure that your cover is visually appealing and accurately represents your book's genre and content. Here are some tips to consider:

1   **Work with a professional designer**: Unless you're a professional designer yourself, it's worth investing in a professional book cover designer. A well-designed cover can make all the difference in attracting readers to your book.

2   **Choose the right images and fonts**: Make sure the images and fonts you choose accurately represent your book's genre and content. Avoid using images or fonts that might be misleading or confusing to potential readers.

3   **Test your cover**: Once you have a design you're happy with, test it out on potential readers to get their feedback. This can help you ensure that your cover is appealing to your target audience.

Pricing and Distribution

The final pieces of metadata to consider are your book's pricing and distribution. Here's what you need to know:

1 **Set the right price**: Do some research to determine the typical price range for books in your genre. You don't want to price your book too high or too low, as either can hurt sales.

2 **Choose your distribution options**: Amazon KDP allows you to distribute your book in multiple formats, including ebooks, print, and audiobooks. Consider which formats are most appropriate for your book and your target audience.

3 **Consider using KDP Select**: KDP Select is a program that allows you to offer your ebook exclusively on Amazon in exchange for certain benefits, such as higher royalties and access to promotional tools. Consider whether this program might be a good fit for your book.

In conclusion, optimizing your book's metadata is crucial to its success on Amazon. By following the steps outlined in this article, you can increase your book's visibility, improve its searchability, and ultimately drive more sales.

If you Buy/Download my Book and found it interesting, I will be glad; if you can leave a nice Review for this book, this will help other potential readers to show interest.

It will take only 30 seconds and it will be greatly appreciated.

Click Here to Leave a Review!

Thank you in advance, I love you and you are the best.

Chapter 6: Standalone verse Series Books and their Benefits

When it comes to publishing books on Amazon Kindle, authors have the option of publishing standalone books or creating a series of books. While standalone books are a great option for some authors, there are many benefits to creating a series of books. In this article, we'll take a look at those benefits and discuss how to create a series of books on Amazon Kindle.

Benefits of Creating a Series of Books

1   Increased Visibility and Sales: Creating a series of books can help increase your visibility on Amazon Kindle. When readers enjoy the first book in a series, they are more likely to look for other books in the series, which can lead to increased sales for the author.

2   Built-in Fan Base: If readers enjoy your first book in a series, they are likely to become fans of your work and eagerly anticipate the release of your next book. This can help build a loyal fan base and make it easier to promote future books.

3   More Opportunities for Marketing: When you have a series of books, you have more opportunities for marketing. You can promote the first book in the series, as well as promote the series as a whole. This can lead to more sales

and increased visibility for your work.

4   Easier to Write: When you have a series of books, you already have a built-in world and characters. This can make it easier to write subsequent books in the series, as you don't have to create everything from scratch.

How to Create a Series of Books on Amazon Kindle

1   **Develop Your Concept:** Before you start writing your series, you need to develop a concept that can sustain multiple books. This could be a world, a set of characters, or a theme. Make sure that your concept is interesting and unique, and something that readers will want to come back to the book after book.

2   **Write Your First Book:** Start by writing your first book in the series. This should be a standalone book that also sets up the world and characters for future books. Make sure that your first book is engaging and leaves readers wanting more.

3   **Plan Your Series:** Once you have written your first book, you should plan out the rest of the series. This can include developing your characters and plot lines for future books, as well as mapping out the overall arc of the series.

4   **Publish Your First Book:** Once you have written and edited your first book, it's time to

publish it on Amazon Kindle. Make sure that you have a strong cover and book description, as well as keywords that will help readers find your book.

5   **Promote Your First Book:** Once your first book is published, you need to promote it. This can include running Amazon ads, reaching out to book bloggers and reviewers, and promoting your book on social media.

6   **Write Subsequent Books:** Once your first book is out and gaining traction, it's time to start writing subsequent books in the series. Make sure that you continue to develop your characters and plot lines, and keep your readers engaged with each new book.

7   **Promote Your Series:** As you publish subsequent books in the series, make sure that you are promoting the series as a whole. This can include running ads that promote the entire series, as well as reaching out to fans and asking them to leave reviews and spread the word about your books.

8   **Friction and Non-Friction Books:** Note that you can write series book on both Friction and Non-Friction books. or noFn-friction books, just make sure the book are related books or beginner to advance and expert book series.

In conclusion, creating a series of books on Amazon

Kindle can be a great way to increase your visibility and sales, build a fan base, and make it easier to write subsequent books. By following the steps outlined above, you can create a successful series that readers will love.

To learn more about the terms and conditions of the amazon series, click below link:
https://kdp.amazon.com/en_US/help/topic/
GMFKBUS43QQ5AJ5A

Chapter 7: Tips to Build an Email List and the Important

When offering your book for free, it's important to ask for something in return, and one effective way is to ask for their email address. You can incentivize this by offering a workbook, a free bonus book, or other related books that may be of interest to the reader. This not only helps you build your email list but also establishes a connection with your readers and shows that you value their support.

Building an email list can be a crucial component of marketing your book and growing your author platform. By collecting email addresses from interested readers, you can stay in touch with them and promote future books, giveaways, and events.

Here are some tips for building an email list and its importance.

1 **Offer something valuable in exchange for their email address:** When offering your book for free, consider asking for something in return, such as the reader's email address. This can help you build an email list of interested readers who are more likely to buy your future books. You can also offer a free workbook or other related books as a bonus for signing up for your email list.

2 **Create an enticing lead magnet:** A lead

magnet is something you offer for free in exchange for a reader's email address. It should be something of value to the reader, such as a free e-book, exclusive content, or access to a private Facebook group. Make sure your lead magnet is relevant to your book and target audience.

3   **Promote your email list on your website and social media:** Make sure your website and social media profiles have clear calls to action for signing up for your email list. You can also use social media ads to promote your lead magnet and email list.

4   **Use an email service provider:** An email service provider can help you manage and automate your email list. It can also provide analytics on email open and click rates, allowing you to better understand your audience and adjust your email marketing strategy accordingly.

5   **Provide valuable content in your emails:** Once you have an email list, it's important to provide valuable content in your emails. This can include exclusive content, behind-the-scenes glimpses into your writing process, or book recommendations. Make sure your emails are well-written, engaging, and relevant to your audience.

6   **Keep your email list engaged:** Regularly

sending emails to your list can help keep them engaged and interested in your work. You can also segment your list based on interests or purchasing behavior to provide more personalized content.

The importance of building an email list lies in its ability to connect you directly with readers who are interested in your work. By nurturing this connection, you can turn readers into fans and fans into loyal customers. An email list can also provide a more reliable source of book sales compared to platforms like social media or book retailers, which are subject to algorithm changes and other factors outside of your control.

In conclusion, building an email list is a valuable tool for authors to connect with readers, promote their work, and increase book sales. By offering something of value in exchange for email addresses, promoting your list on your website and social media, using an email service provider, providing valuable content in your emails, and keeping your list engaged, you can build a loyal audience of readers who are eager to support your writing career.

Also note that this is a long term process, nevertheless incorporate it into your book strategies.

Use can Signup with any the below Email Marketing Programs to Manage your Email List

----

- **Click Here: https://www.getresponse.com/?a=p3PVFhcAEX**
- **Or use Code: p3PVFhcAEX**

- **Click Here: https://www.benchmarkemail.com?partner=1545782**
- **Or Use Partner ID: 1545782**

"**Disclaimer:** Some of the links on this page are affiliate links, and at no additional cost to you, I will earn a commission if you decide to make a purchase. Please understand that I have personal experience with these products and I recommend them because I believe they are helpful and useful, not because of the small commissions I make if you decide to buy something. Please do not spend any money on these products unless you feel you need them or that they will help you achieve your goals. Thank you for supporting my channel."

Chapter 8: The Only Reason you should Giveaway your books

There should be only 1st 3 Reasons to give away your Books.

1. **To Rank your Book:** The 1st Reason is to Rank on Amazon Free Best Seller List. This list is separate from the paid bestseller list and can help increase visibility and generate buzz for your book. By giving away your book for free, you can encourage more downloads and increase your chances of ranking on this list.

2. **To Build your Email List:** Each time your run a free promotion on your books, makc sure you are giving away Bonuses and Other Free Items that will prompt the Readers to Submit their Email Addresses in return for your Promise, that way you can start building your email list. Before you start giving away your book, make sure you have signup for an email newsletter or email marketing platform that will help build your email list, organise them, and even help you build an automated system to do follow-ups on the readers that submit their emails. Therefore includes Links in your kindle ebooks, that will take the readers to where they can email their emails and receive their free bonuses and e-gifts. This can help you build a list of engaged readers who are interested in your work and may be more

likely to buy your future books.

3. **Ask for Review:** another reason you should give away your books is to ask for Reviews. Reviews are crucial for building credibility and increasing sales on Amazon. By giving away your book for free and asking readers to leave a review in exchange, you can quickly accumulate a large number of reviews that can help boost your book's visibility and sales.

Always include a link back to your ebook, so that when they click on it, it will take them back to your book and they can leave a nice review for you. Ask politely and try to do that in 2-3 places/pages in your book: at the beginning, in the middle, and at the end of the book.

It's important to note that giving away your book for free should not be a long-term strategy. While it can be effective in the short term for achieving the above goals, it's ultimately not sustainable for building a profitable writing career.

Instead, use free promotions strategically and sparingly, and focus on building a strong author platform, honing your craft, and promoting your books through other means such as advertising and networking.

When planning a free promotion, be sure to set clear goals and strategies for achieving them. Consider partnering with book bloggers or other influencers to help spread the word about your book, and make sure to track your results carefully to see what's working and what's not.

In conclusion, giving away your book for free can be a powerful way to increase visibility, build your email list, and accumulate reviews. However, it should be used strategically and sparingly, and should not be relied upon as a long-term strategy for building a profitable writing career. By focusing on building a strong author platform, honing your craft, and promoting your books through a variety of channels, you can achieve lasting success as a self-published author.

Chapter 9: How to Get 1st 1000 Sales and more than 50 Reviews

Getting sales on Amazon is the most difficult task in the world, I know, I have been here, forget about all those books you read because you yourself have tried all those things they teach and also most of them are not working.

To sell your book in the first place, you need to write books that people are searching for, you need to write books that readers are willing to pay for, then you need to books with a good title and cover designs.

Now if you have done all the above, the most effective way readers are going to find your books in the first place is by promoting of your book; amazon offers two ways to promote your book which are Free and Paid Promotion.

- **If you don't know how to use them, it will not work.**
- **if you don't know how to use Free Promotions, you will get frustrated.**
- **If you don't know how to use Paid Promotion, you will get burnt; you will send hundreds or thousands of Dollars with low or no success.**

Of course, you need to use the Promotion Ads that Amazon offers you to promote your books, if you want to get your 1st 1000 sales and more reviews.

But you must know that selling on Amazon is an Art or skill, otherwise, it won't work.

Option 1:

- **First Test if the reader wants your book, by using Free Promotion.** If your book gets up to 50 and above orders, then it means your book is desirable.
- **Can readers pay for your Book?** If during Free Promotion, your book got read by Kindle Unlimited Readers and you get paid for it, then that is a sign that people will pay for the book, if you don't get Kindle Unlimited Readers to read your book chances are that book may not get any sales even if you use Paid Promotion.
- **Use Paid Ads.** Now if after your Free Promotion period has expired for the next 90 days, you can use Paid Ads to Boost your Sales, I will advise running a paid ad on books that got some Kindle Unlimited Reads
- After 90 days of the First Free Promotion, you can use the Count Down Promotion + Paid Ad to generate More Sales. Remember to use the Count Down Promotion, don't change your book price for the next 30 days.

Option 2:

- **Use Series Books.** You can use Series to achieve similar things if you don't want to use Paid Ads. I know, I have been there too, burn all your Dollars with Amazon Paid Ads, and you are not getting results but rather losing lots of money.
- **Write your books in series format.** You can have a book series that contains 5 to 20 books. Please check out Amazon Rules and Regulations on Series Books, so that you violate those rules and get your books or series disabled.
- **With 5 to 20 books,** make sure the books are related as much as possible.
- **Then for each book in the series, run 5 days of Free Promotion after each order,** since you only have 5 days of free promotion for the next 90 days, with more books in the series, it will help you expose other books when you have or have not their Free Promotion.
- **Because series Books are chained together when you are running a free promotion on each one of them, readers will also see that you have other books,** and if they are interested, they can also pay to buy the other book that you are running a free promotion on it.
- **With 5 to 20 books in one series, you can spread the Free Promotions to last for that 90 days cycle,** after that you can continue a new cycle with each of the books in that series.

Remember I told you that selling on Amazon is an Art and Skill?

Now let me give you an example: let's say you have 5 books in a particular Series. Then you run a Free Promotion on one of the Books. you can choose to run 2 days free promotion, if that book is getting Kindle unlimited reads, then you know that people can pay for that book.

In another scenario, if another book in that series that you are not running the free promotion on it, is generating sales too, know that readers will also pay for that book.

So with this, you wait for the book that is generating paid reads to be ready after 30 days from the last date you upload the book or change the price to be qualified for Count Promotion. You can then use Paid Ad + Free Count Down Promotion to generate more sales.

If you get more sales, your book can rank for Best Seller, which is a plus for you, remember this strategy is not for you to make more money but to rank your book, get more reviews as possible, and in long run continue to make more sales.

After the Free Count Down Promotion, it will take another 15 days before you can alter the price of that book as amazon will not allow you to change the price, even if you want to.

So in the next 15 days after the end of the countdown

promotion, you can continue with the paid ad if you are still getting more sales from the book

Option 3:

- **Use PermFree and Paid Series Books**
- **This method allows you to set up your 1st book in the series for free permanently to $0.00** and the rest to the prices of your choice.
- **Since you can't set up your book free for free on amazon, you can use other platforms to do so,** and send a request to amazon to match the price of your kindle ebook to $0.00 to be the same as your ebook on other platforms.
- **After Amazon has done so, you can then use Amazon Free promotion to promote the 1st book in the series.**
- **Here is the Sweet part of it,** if you have tested all the books in your series, and some of them got bought or Unlimited Readers read your book, that is a sign that the books in your series will make sales.
- **Then Proceed to use Paid Ad with the PermFree book,** this will draw lots of readers to see your books, they can download the free book and even buy any of the books in your series.

Below are some other Platforms you can upload your book on and set it to $0.00

- Draft2Digital
- Smashwords
- BookFunnel

- Gumroad
- Instafreebie (now Prolific Works)

- Click here to **Download** the **Workbook** that contains **How To Signup On to These Platforms, Upload Your Ebook, And Link Them To Amazon**

- Or Check Toward The End Of The Page To See **How To Signup On to These Platforms, Upload Your Ebook, And Link Them To Amazon**

Chapter 10: How to Ask for Reviews

It's important to ask readers for reviews, but many authors fail to do so in their free books. **Without a clear request, readers may not feel motivated to leave a review.** To avoid this, include the Review Request in 1 to 3 pages in your book asking for reviews politely. These request can be placed at the beginning of the book; after the introduction or first chapter, and/or in the middle of the book, and/or at the end. Be sure to use your own words and provide a compelling reason for readers to leave a review for you and your book. This will not only help you receive valuable feedback but also increase your book's visibility to potential readers and enhance your sales.

As a Kindle author, it's important to understand the power of book reviews. Positive reviews not only encourage other readers to purchase your book, but they also increase your book's visibility on Amazon's search results. However, asking readers for reviews can be a daunting task. In this chapter, we will discuss effective strategies for asking for reviews for your Kindle book.

1. **Include a Call to Action in Your Book:** One of the best ways to encourage readers to leave a review is to include a call to action (CTA) in your book. Adding the request message to the beginning, middle, and end of

your book is a great way to remind readers to leave a review. Your message should be friendly, genuine, and appreciative. Use your own words to make it unique to the type of book you're writing.

- Here are a few examples:
- **At the beginning:** "Thank you for choosing my book. If you enjoy it, I kindly ask that you leave a review. Your feedback will help other readers decide if this book is right for them. Click here to leave a review."

- **In the middle:** "I'm glad you're enjoying my book so far! If you have a few minutes, I would be grateful if you could leave a review. Your review can help other readers make a decision. Click here to leave a review."

- **At the end:** "Congratulations on finishing my book! I hope you found it enjoyable and informative. If you could take a moment to leave a review, I would greatly appreciate it. Your review will help other readers discover my book. Click here to leave a review."

2. **Follow up with Your Readers:** After a reader finishes your book, you can follow up with them and kindly ask for a review. You can do this by sending them an email or a message through your author page on

Amazon. Be sure to thank them for reading your book and politely ask if they would consider leaving a review. Remember, never pressure your readers to leave a review, but instead kindly remind them of the importance of reviews and how it can benefit other readers.

3. **Engage with Your Readers on Social Media:** Social media platforms are great for connecting with your readers and building a relationship with them. You can use social media to ask for reviews by creating a post and kindly asking your followers to leave a review. Be sure to add a link to your book's review page to make it easy for readers to leave a review. You can also create a hashtag for your book and ask readers to use it when leaving a review.

4. **Offer a Free Copy of Your Book:** Offering a free copy of your book in exchange for a review can be an effective strategy for getting more reviews.

You can do this by hosting a giveaway on your website or social media platforms. Make it clear that in exchange for a free copy, you would appreciate an honest review. However, be sure to follow Amazon's guidelines on reviews, which states that reviews should be honest and unbiased.

In conclusion, asking for reviews is an essential part of

promoting your Kindle book. By including a call to action in your book, following up with your readers, engaging with your readers on social media, and offering a free copy of your book, you can increase your chances of getting more reviews. Remember, be genuine, kind, and appreciative when asking for reviews. Good luck!

Chapter 11: Pricing Strategies

Pricing is not much important, if your book title, cover, and table of content is not interesting and compelling, chances are no one will buy your book whether you price it at $0.99, $4.99, $9.99, etc

I have experimented with various pricing, and know you too might also do that, first the topic and title you are writing for, is what will make you sell more, also you can do keyword research of what people are searching for and write your own version on that subject matter. And most importantly I will conclude that whatever price you give your readers, if the topic is important to the readers, they will pay any amount to give your book.

Pricing your book can be a tricky proposition for self-published authors. While it's true that pricing alone won't necessarily make or break your book's success, it's still an important factor to consider when launching and promoting your book.

Here are some key pricing strategies to keep in mind:

1. **Know your audience:** Before setting a price for your book, it's important to understand who your target audience is and what they are willing to pay for books in your

genre. Do some research on other books in your category and see what prices they are selling for. This can help you determine a price point that is competitive and attractive to your potential readers.

2. **Experiment with different prices:** It's also a good idea to experiment with different price points to see what works best for your book. Try pricing your book at different levels, such as $0.99, $2.99, $4.99, and $9.99, and see how sales and revenue are affected. Keep in mind that different price points may work better for different genres and types of books, so be willing to adjust your strategy based on what you learn.

3. **Consider bundling:** Another pricing strategy to consider is bundling your book with other related content or bonuses. This can help justify a higher price point and provide added value to your readers. For example, you might bundle a workbook or companion guide with your book, or offer access to an online course or community.

4. **Don't undervalue your work:** While it's important to be competitive with your pricing, it's also important not to undervalue your work. If you price your book too low, readers may perceive it as lower quality or not worth their time. Remember that writing and publishing a book is a significant

accomplishment, and you should price your work accordingly.

Ultimately, the most important factor in pricing your book is the value it provides to your readers. If you've created a compelling title, cover, and table of contents, and you've targeted your audience effectively, readers will be willing to pay a fair price for your work. Be willing to experiment with different pricing strategies, but always keep the needs and interests of your readers in mind.

Chapter 12: Promote your Other Books in your Book

When distributing your book for free or in all of your books, consider including the title, cover, and link to your other books. By doing this, readers may become interested in your other works and click the provided link to learn more. If they find your book description and price appealing, they may go on to purchase your other books.

Here are the steps to take to effectively promote your other books in your Kindle book:

Step 1: Identify Your Other Books: Identify the other books you want to promote in your Kindle book. Choose books that are related to your current book or target the same audience, and make sure they are available on Amazon.

Step 2: Create a Compelling Call-to-Action: Create a compelling call-to-action (CTA) that encourages readers to check out your other books. Your CTA should be clear, concise, and placed strategically in your book. Consider using images of your book covers and adding hyperlinks to make it easier for readers to click through to your other books.

Step 3: Include Book Samples: Include samples of your other books in your Kindle book. This gives readers a taste of your writing style and encourages them to check out your other work. Consider including the first chapter or a few pages of your other books at the end of your current book.

Step 4: Use Keywords and Categories: Use relevant keywords and categories when listing your other books on Amazon. This helps them appear in search results when readers are looking for similar books.

Step 5: Offer Discounts and Promotions: Offer discounts and promotions on your other books to incentivize readers to buy them. You can use Amazon's Kindle Countdown Deals or run your own promotions on your website or social media channels.

Step 6: Update Your Books Regularly: Make sure to update your Kindle books regularly with new information, links, and promotions for your other books. This keeps your readers engaged and increases the chances of them checking out your other work.

By following these steps, you can effectively promote your other books in your Kindle book and increase your chances of generating more sales. Remember to focus on providing value to your readers and making it easy for them to learn more about your other work. Always be willing to adjust and improve your promotional efforts based on their feedback and needs.

If you Buy/Download my Book and found it interesting, I will be glad; if you can leave a nice Review for this book, this will help other potential readers to show interest.

It will take only 30 seconds and it will be greatly appreciated.

Click Here to Leave a Review!

Thank you in advance, I love you and you are the best.

Chapter 13: Link your Amazon Author in your Book

Linking your Amazon Author page to your Kindle book can help readers learn more about you as an author and discover other books you have written. Here are the steps to link your Amazon Kindle Author in your book:

Step 1: Create Your Amazon Author Page: If you have not already created your Amazon Author Page, follow these steps:

1. Go to https://authorcentral.amazon.com/ and sign in with your Amazon account.

2. Follow the instructions to complete your author profile, including adding a bio, author photo, and any books you have published.

3. Once you have completed your profile, click on the "Profile" tab at the top of the page to view your Author Page.

Step 2: Find Your Kindle Book on Amazon: Log in to your Amazon KDP (Kindle Direct Publishing) account and navigate to your book's detail page on Amazon.

Step 3: Get Your Book's ASIN or ISBN: On your book's detail page, scroll down to the "Product details" section. Look for the "ASIN" or "ISBN" number, which is a unique identifier for your book.

Step 4: Add Your Author Page URL to Your Book's Metadata and inside your books: In your Amazon KDP account, go to the "Bookshelf" tab and click on the title of the book you want to link to your Author Page.

1. Scroll down to the "Book Details" section and click on the "Edit" button next to "Contributors."

2. In the "Contributor Roles" section, select "Author" from the drop-down menu.

3. In the "Author Biography" section, paste the URL for your Amazon Author Page in the "Author Central URL" field.

4. Click "Save and Continue" to save your changes.

Step 5: Verify Your Author Page Link: After saving your changes, Amazon may take up to 72 hours to process the link between your book and your author page. To verify that the link is working:

1. Go to your book's detail page on Amazon and scroll down to the "Product details" section.

2. Look for the "Author" section, which should include your name as a link to your author page.

3. Click on your name to verify that the link takes you to your author page.

In conclusion, linking your Amazon Author Page to your Kindle book can help readers discover more about you as an author and find other books you have written. By following these steps, you can easily add your author page URL to your book's metadata and verify that the link is working properly. Remember to keep your author page up-to-date with new books and information about yourself as an author to engage and connect with your readers.

Chapter 14: Finding a Profitable Niche for Your Kindle Book

Finding a profitable niche for your Kindle book is crucial to its success. Here are the steps to take to find a niche
with less than 1000 results on Amazon and maximize your chances of generating more sales:

Step 1: Identify Your Interests and Expertise: Start by identifying your interests and areas of expertise. Look for topics you are passionate about and have knowledge and experience in. This will help you write a book that provides value to your readers and establishes you as an authority in your niche.

Step 2: Research Popular and Trending Niches: Research popular and trending niches on Amazon, and look for gaps in the market that you can fill. Use Amazon's Best Sellers Rank, category rankings, and customer reviews to get a sense of what's selling and what readers are looking for.

Step 3: Analyze the Competition: Analyze the competition in your chosen niche and look for books with less than 1000 results on Amazon. Check their covers, titles, descriptions, and reviews to get a sense of what's working and what's not. Look for ways to differentiate your book from theirs and provide unique value to your readers.

Step 4: Narrow Down Your Niche: Once you have a list of potential niches, narrow them down based on their profitability, competition, and potential for growth. Look for niches with high demand and low competition, and make sure there is enough market potential to support your book.

Step 5: Validate Your Niche: Before you start writing your book, validate your niche by conducting keyword research and testing the market with a minimum viable product (MVP). Use keyword research tools to see how many people are searching for your niche, and test the market with a short e-book or blog post to see if there is enough interest and demand for your topic.

By following these steps, you can find a profitable niche with less than 1000 results on Amazon and increase your chances of getting found by readers and generating more sales. Remember to focus on providing value to your readers, and always be willing to adjust and improve your book based on their feedback and needs.

Chapter 15: Keyword Research - How to Find the Right Keywords to Optimize Your Book for Search

Keyword research is a critical aspect of optimizing your book for search and increasing its visibility on Amazon.

Here are the steps to take to find the right keywords for your book:

Step 1: Brainstorm Keywords: Start by brainstorming a list of keywords that are relevant to your book's topic and target audience. Think about the words and phrases people would use to search for your book on Amazon.

Step 2: Use Amazon's Autocomplete Feature: Amazon's Autocomplete feature can help you generate more keyword ideas and see what other people are searching for related to your book. Simply type in a keyword related to your book, and Amazon will suggest related searches.

Step 3: Use Keyword Research Tools: Keyword research tools like Google Keyword Planner or Ubersuggest can help you find more targeted and high-traffic keywords related to your book. These tools can also provide valuable insights into search volume, competition, and trends.

Step 4: Analyze Your Competitors' Keywords: Analyzing your competitors' keywords can give you a better understanding of what keywords are working for them and how you can differentiate your book from theirs. Look at the titles, subtitles, and descriptions of books in your niche that are ranking well, and see what keywords they are using.

Step 5: Choose the Right Keywords: Once you have a list of potential keywords, choose the ones that are most relevant and targeted to your book's topic and audience. Use these keywords in your book's title, subtitle, and description to optimize it for search.

Step 6: Monitor Your Results: Finally, it's essential to monitor your book's performance regularly and track the impact of your keyword optimization efforts. Use analytics tools to monitor your sales, click-through rates, and other key metrics to help you make data-driven decisions about your book's marketing and promotion.

By following these steps, you can find the right keywords to optimize your book for search, increase its visibility on Amazon, and generate more sales. Remember to focus on providing value to your target audience through your book and marketing efforts, and always be willing to experiment and adjust your strategies as needed.

Chapter 16: Things that Hurts your Book Ranking

As an author, it's important to understand the factors that affect your book ranking on Amazon. While there are many things that can impact your book's visibility and sales, one of the most common mistakes authors make is constantly changing their book pricing.

Each time you make a change to your book's pricing, Amazon will view your book as a new release. This means that it will take time for your book to regain its previous rankings, and this can be detrimental to your overall sales.

Another factor that can impact your book ranking is the way you structure your series books. If you plan to create a series, it's important to decide how many books will be in the series and the pricing of each book before you publish the first book.

When you add or reshuffle books in a series, it can affect the rankings of all the books in that series. This is because Amazon views each book in a series as interconnected and evaluates the sales and reviews of each book when determining the overall ranking of the series.

So, it's important to plan ahead and think about the long-term strategy for your book series. Make sure you have a clear plan for the number of books you want to write and the pricing for each book. This will help you maintain consistency and prevent any negative impact on your book's ranking.

Another factor that can hurt your book's ranking is poor reviews. If your book has a low rating or negative reviews, it can affect your overall sales and visibility on Amazon. To prevent this, make sure you have quality content, editing, and proofreading before publishing your book.

Additionally, it's important to engage with your readers and encourage them to leave reviews. This can be done through a simple request at the end of your book or through email follow-ups with your readers.

Another mistake that can hurt your book ranking is poor formatting. If your book is difficult to read or contains formatting errors, it can negatively impact your reader's experience and lead to negative reviews.

Make sure your book is properly formatted before publishing, and consider hiring a professional formatter if you're not confident in your formatting skills. A well-formatted book will help your readers stay engaged and prevent any negative impact on your book's ranking.

In conclusion, maintaining a consistent pricing strategy, planning ahead for series books, and ensuring quality content and formatting are all important factors in maintaining a good book ranking on Amazon. By taking the time to plan and prepare, you can improve your book's visibility and sales over time.

Chapter 17: The Importance of having your own website as a Kindle Author

As a Kindle author, having your own website can be a powerful tool to help you build your brand, connect with readers, and sell more books. In this step-by-step guide, we'll explore why having a website is important, what you need to do to get started, and how to make the most of your site once it's up and running.

Part 1: Why You Need a Website

1. **Build Your Brand:** Your website is a hub for your brand. It's the place where readers can come to learn more about you, your books, and your writing process. Your website should be a reflection of your personality and your writing style. The design, layout, and content should all be consistent with your brand.

2. **Connect With Readers:** Your website is a great place to connect with your readers. You can use your website to interact with your readers, share your writing process, and promote your books. By interacting with your readers, you can build a loyal following and turn casual readers into devoted fans.

3. **Sell More Books:** Your website can be a

powerful sales tool. You can use your website to sell your books directly to readers, offer special deals and promotions, and build a mailing list to keep readers updated on your latest releases. By selling your books directly, you can also earn more money per sale than you would through a third-party retailer like Amazon.

Part 2: Getting Started

1. Choose a Domain Name: Your domain name is the address people will use to find your website. Choose a name that is easy to remember and easy to spell. Ideally, your domain name should be your author name, but if that's not available, choose a name that is closely related to your brand.

2. Choose a Hosting Service: A hosting service is a company that provides the server space and technology needed to run your website. There are many hosting services available, but some of the most popular include Bluehost, SiteGround, HostGator and **InterServer.** Choose a hosting service that fits your budget and offers the features you need. **I recommend you use InterServer for the Affordable Unlimited Swift Domain Registration and Hosting Services.**

3. Choose a Content Management System: A

content management system (CMS) is software that helps you manage the content on your website. There are many CMS options available, but some of the most popular include WordPress, Joomla, and Drupal. Choose a CMS that is easy to use and offers the features you need.

4. Design Your Site: Once you have your domain name, hosting service, and CMS, it's time to design your site. You can use a pre-made template or hire a web designer to create a custom design. Your site should be visually appealing, easy to navigate, and consistent with your brand.

Part 3: Making the Most of Your Site

1. **Create a Blog:** Your blog is a great place to share your writing process, connect with your readers, and promote your books. Your blog posts should be informative, engaging, and consistent with your brand.

2. **Sell Your Books:** Your website is a great place to sell your books directly to readers. You can use a plugin like WooCommerce or Easy Digital Downloads to set up a shopping cart and accept payments. Make sure to include detailed descriptions and cover images for each of your books.

3. **Build a Mailing List:** A mailing list is a powerful tool for building a loyal following and promoting your books. You can use a service like MailChimp or Constant Contact to manage your list and send out newsletters and promotional emails.

4. **Optimize for Search Engines:** Search engine optimization (SEO) is the process of optimizing your site so it appears higher in search engine rankings. You can improve your site's SEO by using keywords in your content, creating high-quality backlinks, and making sure your site is mobile-friendly.

5. **Promote Your Site:** Once your website is up and running, it's important to promote it to attract visitors. You can use social media platforms like Facebook, Twitter, and Instagram to promote your site and your books. You can also participate in online forums and communities related to your genre to connect with potential readers.

6. **Analyze Your Traffic:** It's important to track the traffic to your website so you can see what's working and what's not. You can use tools like Google Analytics to track the number of visitors to your site, where they're coming from, and

what pages they're visiting. This information can help you make informed decisions about how to improve your site and your promotional efforts.

7. **Update Your Site Regularly:** Finally, it's important to update your site regularly with new content to keep readers coming back. You can use your blog to share updates on your writing process, book releases, and promotional events. You can also share guest posts and interviews with other authors to provide valuable content for your readers.

In conclusion, having your own website as a Kindle author can be a powerful tool to help you build your brand, connect with readers, and sell more books. By following the steps outlined in this guide, you can create a website that reflects your brand and provides a platform to promote your writing.

Remember to update your site regularly and track your traffic to make informed decisions about how to improve your site and your promotional efforts. With a well-designed website and effective promotion, you can turn casual readers into devoted fans and build a successful career as a Kindle author.

Chapter 18: How to Use Social Media Platforms to Promote your Book

Social media platforms are a great way to promote your Kindle books and reach a wider audience. Here are some tips on how to use social media to promote your books:

1. **Choose the Right Platforms:** There are many social media platforms available, but not all of them are right for promoting your books. Choose platforms that are popular among readers in your genre. For example, if you write romance novels, you may want to focus on Facebook, Instagram, and Pinterest. If you write thrillers, you may want to focus on Twitter and Reddit.

2. **Build Your Profile:** Your social media profile is the first thing people see when they visit your page. Make sure your profile is complete and includes a bio, profile picture, and cover image. Use a professional headshot for your profile picture and choose a cover image that reflects your brand.

3. **Engage With Your Followers:** Social media is all about engagement. Take the time to respond to comments and messages from your

followers. Ask questions and start conversations to encourage engagement. This will help you build a loyal following and turn casual readers into devoted fans.

4. **Share Content:** Social media is all about sharing content. Share photos, videos, and blog posts that are related to your books and your brand. This can include updates on your writing process, book covers, and reviews. Share content from other authors and publishers to provide value to your followers.

5. **Run Promotions:** Social media is a great place to run promotions and giveaways. Offer free copies of your book or other prizes to encourage engagement and build your following. Make sure to follow the rules and guidelines of the platform you're using.

6. **Use Hashtags:** Hashtags are a great way to reach a wider audience on social media. Use relevant hashtags to make it easier for readers to find your posts. You can also create your own hashtag to build brand awareness and encourage engagement. Use Trending hashtag to reach to more people who are online and may be interested in you book.

7. **Advertise:** If you have a budget, consider using

social media advertising to promote your books. Most social media platforms offer advertising options that allow you to target specific audiences based on demographics and interests.

8. **Be Consistent:** Finally, be consistent with your social media activity. Post regularly and engage with your followers on a consistent basis. This will help you build a strong following and keep your brand top of mind with your audience.

In conclusion, social media is a powerful tool for promoting your Kindle books and reaching a wider audience. By following these tips, you can build a strong social media presence and connect with readers in your genre. Remember to be consistent, engage with your followers, and share valuable content to build a loyal following and turn casual readers into devoted fans.

Chapter 19: How to Use YouTube Videos to Generate Traffic to your Book

YouTube is the second-largest search engine in the world, making it an excellent platform for authors to promote their Kindle books. Here are some tips on how to use YouTube videos to generate traffic to your Kindle book:

1. **Create a Book Trailer:** A book trailer is a short video that introduces your book to potential readers. It can be an effective way to create buzz around your book and generate interest. Your book trailer should be visually appealing and highlight the key themes and characters of your book. Make sure to include a call to action at the end of the video to encourage viewers to check out your book.

2. **Create Informational Videos:** Informational videos are another great way to promote your book on YouTube. You can create videos that provide background information on your book, like how you came up with the idea or what inspired you to write it. You can also create videos that provide tips and advice related to the themes of your book.

3. **Share Excerpts:** You can also share excerpts

from your book in a video format. This is a great way to give readers a taste of your writing style and get them interested in your book. Make sure to include a call to action at the end of the video to encourage viewers to check out the full book.

4. **Use Keywords:** Just like with written content, keywords are important for YouTube videos. Use relevant keywords in your video title, description, and tags to make it easier for viewers to find your video. You can use tools like Google AdWords Keyword Planner to find relevant keywords.

5. **Cross-Promote:** Cross-promoting your YouTube videos on your social media platforms and website can help generate more views and traffic. Encourage your followers to share your videos and provide a link to your book in the video description.

6. **Engage with Viewers:** Engage with your viewers by responding to comments and questions. This can help build a community around your book and encourage viewers to share your video.

7. **Analyze Your Data:** Use YouTube's analytics tool to track the performance of your videos. This can help you identify which videos are

performing well and which ones need improvement. Use this data to improve your future videos and promotional efforts.

In conclusion, YouTube can be an effective platform for promoting your Kindle book. By creating book trailers, informational videos, and sharing excerpts, you can generate buzz and interest around your book. Use keywords, cross-promote, and engage with viewers to increase visibility and traffic. Remember to analyze your data to improve your future videos and promotional efforts. With consistent effort and quality content, you can use YouTube to connect with potential readers and sell more Kindle books.

To Create YouTube Videos as Beginner, you can these Top AI Video Creation Online Tools

----

"**Disclaimer:** Some of the links on this page are affiliate links, and at no additional cost to you, I will earn a commission if you decide to make a purchase. Please understand that I have personal experience with these products and I recommend them because I believe they are helpful and useful, not because of the small commissions I make if you decide to buy something. Please do not spend any money on these products unless you feel you need them or that they will help you achieve your goals. Thank you for supporting my channel."

Click Direct: https://pictory.ai/?ref=okade47
Or Use My Code: okade47

Click Direct: https://www.synthesia.io/?
via=christopher-okade
Or Use My Code: christopher-okade

Click Direct: https://murf.ai/?lmref=hzYcYA
Or Use My Code: hzYcYA

Chapter 20: Selling on other Platforms

There are several other platforms where you can sell your eBooks and paperback books apart from Amazon KDP. Some of these platforms include:

1. **Barnes & Noble Press:** This platform allows authors to sell their eBooks and paperbacks on the Barnes & Noble website.

2. **Kobo Writing Life:** Kobo is a Canadian eBook retailer that allows authors to publish and sell their eBooks on their platform.

3. **Apple Books:** Apple Books is an eBook store for iOS devices where authors can sell their eBooks.

4. **Google Play Books:** Google Play Books is an eBook store where authors can sell their eBooks to readers who use Android devices.

5. **Smashwords:** Smashwords is an eBook publishing and distribution platform that allows authors to sell their eBooks on multiple retailers, including Apple Books, Barnes & Noble, Kobo, and others.

6. **Draft2Digital:** Draft2Digital is a platform that allows authors to publish their eBooks and paperbacks on multiple retailers, including

Apple Books, Barnes & Noble, Kobo, and others.

7   **BookBaby:** BookBaby is a platform that allows authors to publish and sell their eBooks and paperbacks on multiple retailers, including Amazon, Barnes & Noble, Kobo, and others.

When choosing a platform to sell your eBooks and paperbacks, it's important to consider the audience you're targeting, the fees involved, and the level of control you'll have over your work. Some platforms may offer more marketing support or higher royalty rates, while others may give you more control over pricing and distribution.

- Click here to **Download** the **Workbook** that contains **How To Signup On to These Platforms, Upload Your Ebook, And Link Them To Amazon**
-
- Or Check Toward The End Of The Page To See **How To Link and Sell your Books on Amazon and other Platforms.**

Chapter 21: How to Use ChatGPT to Speedup Book Upload and Promotion

Signup or Login to ChatGPT https://chat.openai.com/chat/

ChatGPT

Examples

"Explain quantum computing in simple terms" →

"Got any creative ideas for a 10 year old's birthday?" →

"How do I make an HTTP request in Javascript?" →

Capabilities

Remembers what user said earlier in the conversation

Allows user to provide follow-up corrections

Trained to decline inappropriate requests

Limitations

May occasionally generate incorrect information

May occasionally produce harmful instructions or biased content

Limited knowledge of world and events after 2021

ChatGPT Promopt

ChatGPT Feb 13 Version. Free Research Preview. Our goal is to make AI systems more natural and safe to interact with. Your feedback will help us improve

Writing a book is an incredible accomplishment, but publishing it can be a daunting task. After pouring your heart and soul into your manuscript, the next step is to promote it to the world. However, book promotion requires a whole different set of skills that many authors may not have. From designing an eye-catching book cover to crafting a compelling Amazon description, there are many elements to consider when promoting your book. This is where ChatGPT comes in. As a large language model, ChatGPT can help you speed up your book upload and promotion process. In this book, we will explore how to use ChatGPT to generate book cover design ideas, write Amazon descriptions and keywords, suggest Amazon categories, and even generate Facebook ads, video trailers, and YouTube video scripts. With these tips and tricks, you can promote your book like a pro and reach a wider audience.

Generating Book Cover Design Ideas

Your book cover is the first thing that readers see, and it can make or break their decision to buy your book. To stand out from the crowd, you need a cover that captures the essence of your book and appeals to your target audience. ChatGPT can help you generate book cover design ideas by analyzing your book's genre, plot, and themes. Simply input your book's details into ChatGPT, and it will generate a list of potential book cover designs for you to choose from. You can then use these designs as inspiration or even as the basis for your book cover.

Crafting Compelling Amazon Descriptions and Keywords

Your Amazon description and keywords are essential for getting your book noticed on Amazon. Your description should be clear, concise, and compelling, and your keywords should accurately reflect the content of your book. ChatGPT can help you write your Amazon description and keywords by analyzing your book's plot, themes, and genre. It can also provide suggestions for related keywords that you may not have considered. With ChatGPT's help, you can create a description and keywords that will attract readers to your book.

Suggesting Amazon Categories

Choosing the right Amazon categories is crucial for getting your book in front of the right audience. However, it can be challenging to navigate Amazon's category system and find the best categories for your book. ChatGPT can help you suggest Amazon categories by analyzing your book's genre and content. It can also provide suggestions for related categories that you may not have considered. With ChatGPT's help, you can choose the best categories for your book and increase your chances of reaching your target audience.

Tips and Tricks for Ranking Your Book in More Categories

Ranking your book in multiple Amazon categories can help you reach a wider audience and increase your book's visibility. However, achieving this can be challenging. ChatGPT can provide tips and tricks for ranking your book in more categories, such as using specific keywords, analyzing your competition, and optimizing your book's metadata. With these strategies, you can increase your book's visibility and reach more readers.

Generating Compelling Facebook Ads or Sales

Pitch

Facebook ads are a great way to promote your book to a targeted audience. However, creating an ad that is both compelling and effective can be challenging. ChatGPT can help you generate a compelling Facebook ad or sales pitch by analyzing your book's plot, themes, and genre. It can also provide suggestions for ad copy and targeting options. With ChatGPT's help, you can create a Facebook ad that will capture the attention of potential readers.

Generating Video Trailer and YouTube Video Scripts

Video trailers and YouTube videos are powerful tools for promoting your book. They allow you to showcase your book in a visually compelling way and reach a wider audience. However, creating a video script can be time-consuming and challenging. ChatGPT can help you generate a video trailer or YouTube script by analyzing your book's plot, themes, and genre. It can also provide suggestions for visuals, voiceover, and music. With ChatGPT's help, you can create a video script that will engage viewers and encourage them to buy your book.

Using ChatGPT to speed up your book upload and promotion process can save you time and energy while also helping you reach a wider audience. From generating book cover design ideas to crafting compelling Amazon descriptions and keywords, ChatGPT can provide valuable insights and suggestions to help you promote your book like a pro.

With the tips and tricks in this book, you can use ChatGPT to increase your book's visibility and reach more readers. Whether you're a first-time author or an experienced writer, this book is a must-read for anyone looking to promote their book with the help of ChatGPT.

Chapter 22: How to Use ChatGPT to generate your Book Cover Design Ideas

Your book cover is the first thing that potential readers see, so it's essential to make a great first impression. A book cover that is eye-catching, compelling, and relevant to the book's content is more likely to grab readers' attention and encourage them to pick up your book. However, designing a book cover can be a daunting task, especially if you're not a graphic designer. This is where ChatGPT comes in. As a large language model, ChatGPT can help you generate book cover design ideas by analyzing your book's genre, plot, and themes. In this section, we'll explore how to use ChatGPT to generate your book cover design ideas step-by-step.

Note: If you have write your book or have at least have all your book chapters or introduction ready. To use ChatGPT generate book design idea, copy the book and and all chapters or copy the book title and the introduction into the ChatGPT Prompt. This will help ChatGPT understand your book idea and it will enable it to give you better results.

Step 1: Input Your Book's Details

The first step in using ChatGPT to generate your book cover design ideas is to input your book's details. This includes the book's title, author name, and a brief description of the book's plot and themes. You can also input the genre of your book, which will help ChatGPT generate more relevant cover designs.

Step 2: Select Your Desired Cover Design Style

ChatGPT can generate book cover designs in various styles, including minimalist, photographic, typographic, and illustrative. Once you have input your book's details, you can select the cover design style that best suits your book's genre and content. For example, a minimalist cover design may be more appropriate for a literary novel, while an illustrative design may be more suitable for a children's book.

Step 3: Choose Your Preferred Color Scheme

The color scheme of your book cover is an important aspect of its overall design. Different colors can convey different moods and emotions, so it's essential to choose a color scheme that is appropriate for your book's content. ChatGPT can generate book cover designs in various color schemes, including monochromatic, complementary, and analogous. Once you have selected your desired cover design style, you can choose your preferred color scheme.

/ 2

Book Title: `How to Be Successful in 5 Years: The Secret of Highest Achievers`.

Chapter 1: Setting Achievable Goals Chapter 2: Developing a Success Mindset
Chapter 3: Building a Strong Work Ethic
Chapter 4: Cultivating Strong Relationships
Chapter 5: Learning from Failure
Chapter 6: Developing Time Management Skills
Chapter 7: Taking Action and Following Through

Give me a Book Cover Design Idea for this book, also suggest compelling Background and Text color and Possible Font for the title and sub-tile, etc

Book Cover Design Idea:
The cover could feature a mountain with a winding path leading up to its peak. At the summit, there could be a silhouette of a person standing triumphantly with arms raised. The image would represent the journey to success, with the path leading up to the peak symbolizing the steps readers can take to achieve their goals.

Background Color: A gradient of blue to represent growth and success, starting with a light blue at the bottom and gradually darkening to a navy blue at the top.

Step 4: Review and Select Your Book Cover Design

After inputting your book's details, selecting your desired cover design style, and choosing your preferred color scheme, ChatGPT will generate a list of potential book cover designs. You can review these designs and select the one that best captures the essence of your book and appeals to your target audience. ChatGPT can generate multiple cover designs, so you can choose the one that you think is the most effective.

Step 5: Use Your Selected Cover Design

Once you have selected your book cover design, you can use it to create your book cover. You can hire a graphic designer to create the cover for you, or you can use a design platform like Canva to create your cover using the selected design as a starting point. Alternatively, you can use the design as inspiration and create your cover from scratch.

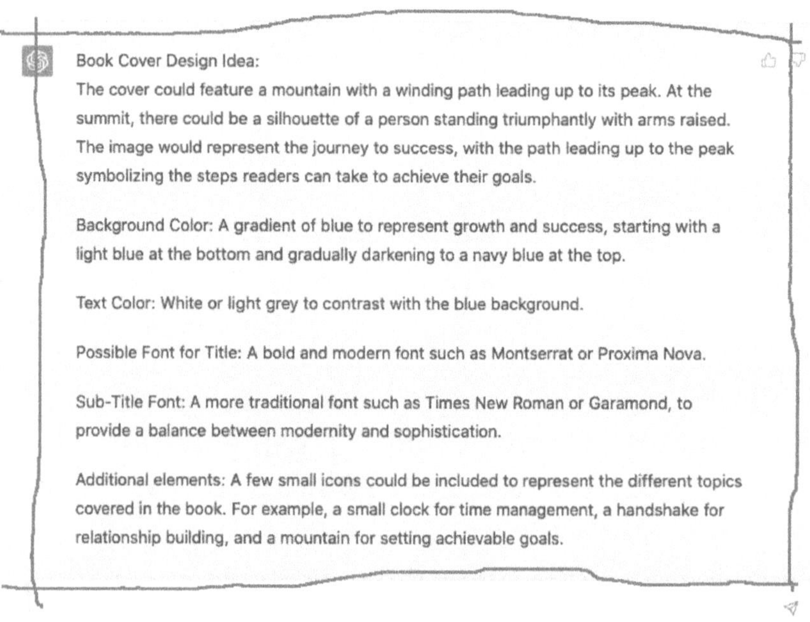

Tips for Using ChatGPT to Generate Book

Cover Design Ideas

Here are some tips for using ChatGPT to generate book cover design ideas effectively:

- Be specific when inputting your book's details. The more information you provide, the more accurate the generated cover designs will be.

- Consider your target audience when selecting your desired cover design style and color scheme. Different genres and demographics respond to different cover designs and color schemes.

- Don't be afraid to experiment with different cover design styles and color schemes. ChatGPT can generate multiple cover designs, so you can choose the one that best represents your book.

- Use the generated cover designs as inspiration, but don't feel constrained by them. You can use the design as a starting point and create your cover from scratch, or you can modify the generated design to suit your preferences.

Conclusion

GPT's help, you can streamline the process and save time while still creating a compelling book cover design. By inputting your book's details, selecting your desired cover design style and color scheme, and reviewing and selecting your preferred design, you can use ChatGPT to generate book cover design ideas that are relevant, engaging, and unique to your book.

Chapter 23: How to Use ChatGPT to write your Book Compelling Amazon Description

Your Amazon book description is one of the most critical elements of your book's marketing. It's your opportunity to grab the reader's attention, convey the key selling points of your book, and convince them to make a purchase. However, writing a compelling book description can be challenging, especially if you're not a skilled copywriter. This is where ChatGPT can help. In this section, we'll explore how to use ChatGPT to write your book's compelling Amazon description step-by-step.

Step 1: Input Your Book's Details

The first step in using ChatGPT to write your book's compelling Amazon description is to input your book's details. This includes the book's title, author name, and a brief summary of the book's plot and themes. You can also input the book's genre, which will help ChatGPT generate more relevant description ideas.

Step 2: Select Your Desired Tone and Style

ChatGPT can generate book descriptions in various

tones and styles, including conversational, informative, and persuasive. Once you have input your book's details, you can select the tone and style that best suits your book's genre and content. For example, a conversational tone may be more appropriate for a memoir, while a persuasive tone may be more suitable for a self-help book.

Step 3: Choose Your Key Selling Points

Your book's key selling points are the features that make it stand out from other books in its genre. This may include the book's unique plot, the author's credentials, or the book's relevance to current events. ChatGPT can help you identify your book's key selling points by analyzing your book's genre and content. Once you have identified your key selling points, you can input them into ChatGPT.

Step 4: Review and Refine Your Book Description

After inputting your book's details, selecting your desired tone and style, and choosing your key selling points, ChatGPT will generate a list of potential book descriptions. You can review these descriptions and refine them to suit your preferences. ChatGPT can generate multiple book descriptions, so you can choose the one that you think is the most effective.

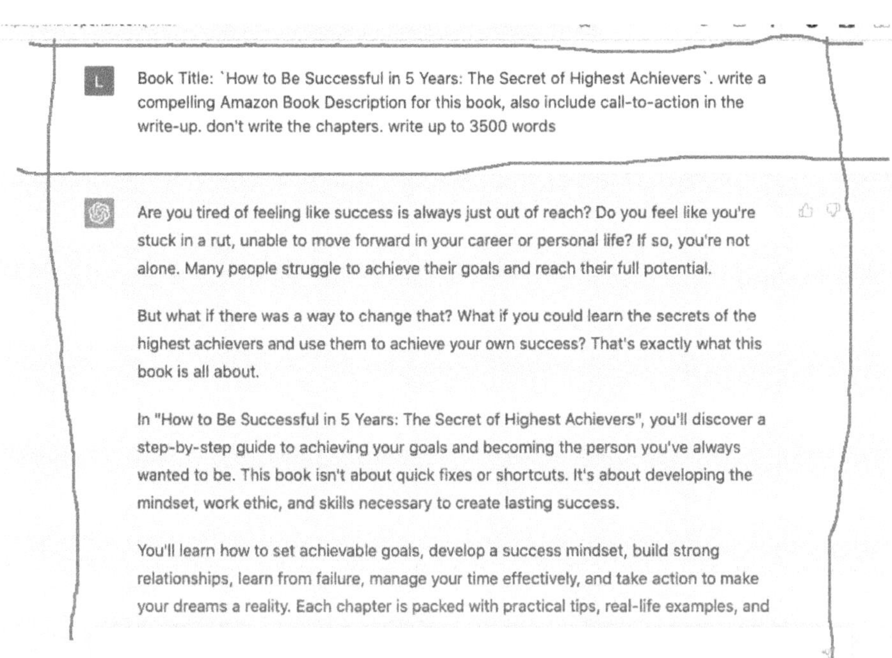

Step 5: Use Your Selected Book Description

Once you have selected your book description, you can use it to create your Amazon book page. You can copy and paste the description into the product description field on your book's Amazon page, or you can use it as inspiration and create your description from scratch.

Tips for Using ChatGPT to Write Your Book's Compelling Amazon Description

Here are some tips for using ChatGPT to write your book's compelling Amazon description effectively:

- Be specific when inputting your book's details. The more information you provide, the more accurate the generated descriptions will be.

- Consider your target audience when selecting your desired tone and style. Different genres and demographics respond to different writing styles and tones.

- Focus on your book's unique selling points. These are the features that will make your book stand out and grab the reader's attention.

- Refine the generated descriptions to suit your preferences. ChatGPT can generate multiple descriptions, so you can choose the one that you think is the most effective and refine it to make it even better.

Conclusion

Writing a compelling Amazon book description is essential for grabbing the reader's attention and convincing them to make a purchase. With ChatGPT's help, you can streamline the process and save time while still creating a description that effectively conveys the key selling points of your book. By inputting your book's details, selecting your desired tone and style, choosing your key selling points, and reviewing and refining your book description, you can use ChatGPT to write a compelling Amazon description that resonates with your target audience.

Chapter 24: How to Use ChatGPT to write your Book Keywords

Choosing the right keywords for your book can be a game-changer when it comes to visibility and discoverability on Amazon. Keywords are words or phrases that readers use when searching for books on Amazon. By using relevant and specific keywords, you can ensure that your book appears in the search results when readers are looking for books in your genre. In this section, we'll explore how to use ChatGPT to write your book keywords step-by-step.

Step 1: Identify Your Book's Genre

The first step in using ChatGPT to write your book keywords is to identify your book's genre. Your book's genre will help you determine which keywords are relevant and specific to your book. For example, if your book is a romance novel, keywords such as "romance," "love story," and "contemporary romance" may be relevant.

Step 2: Input Your Book's Details

Once you have identified your book's genre, the next step is to input your book's details into ChatGPT. This includes your book's title, author name, and a brief summary of your book's plot and themes. You can also input your book's genre to help ChatGPT generate more relevant keyword ideas.

Step 3: Use ChatGPT to Generate Keyword Ideas

ChatGPT can generate a list of potential keywords for your book based on the information you input. The keywords can include specific phrases, such as "historical romance" or "paranormal romance," or general terms like "bestseller" or "must-read." The list of keywords generated will depend on the information you input, including your book's genre, themes, and characters.

Step 4: Analyze and Refine Your Keywords

Once ChatGPT has generated a list of potential keywords for your book, it's time to analyze and refine the list. Review the list of keywords and select the ones that are most relevant to your book. Look for keywords that have high search volume and low competition, as these are more likely to drive traffic to your book's page. You can use keyword research tools like Google AdWords or KDP Rocket to help you identify high-volume and low-competition keywords.

Step 5: Use Your Selected Keywords

After you have analyzed and refined your list of keywords, it's time to use them. You can include your selected keywords in your book's title, subtitle, and book description on Amazon. You can also include them in your book's metadata when you upload it to

KDP. By using relevant and specific keywords, you can ensure that your book appears in the search results when readers are looking for books in your genre.

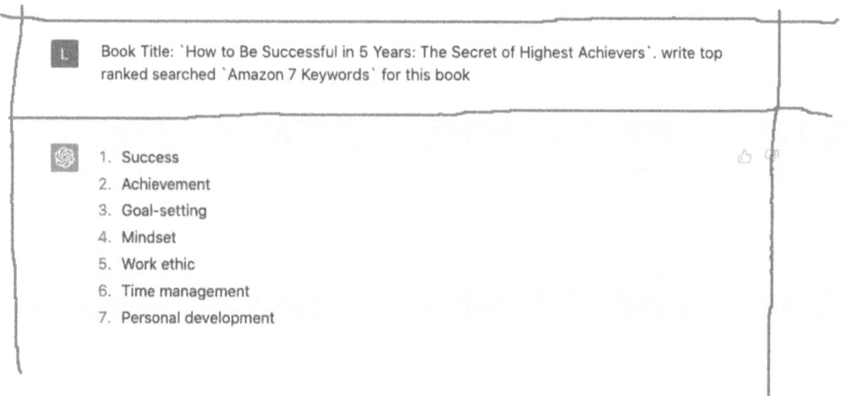

Tips for Using ChatGPT to Write Your Book Keywords

Here are some tips for using ChatGPT to write your book keywords effectively:

- Be specific when inputting your book's details. The more information you provide, the more accurate the generated keywords will be.

- Use specific keywords that are relevant to your book's genre, themes, and characters. General keywords like "book" or "novel" are too broad and won't help your book stand out in the search results.

- Look for high-volume, low-competition keywords. These are the keywords that are most likely to drive traffic to your book's page.

- Use keyword research tools like Google AdWords or KDP Rocket to help you identify high-volume and low-competition keywords.

Conclusion

Choosing the right keywords for your book is crucial for visibility and discoverability on Amazon. By using ChatGPT to generate keyword ideas based on your book's genre, themes, and characters, you can ensure that your book appears in the search results when readers are looking for books in your genre. By refining your list of keywords and using them in your book's title, subtitle, and book description, you can increase your book's visibility and attract more potential readers. Remember to analyze and refine your keyword list regularly to ensure that you are using the most effective keywords for your book. By following these steps and tips, you can use ChatGPT to write your book keywords and improve your book's chances of success on Amazon.

Chapter 25: How to Use ChatGPT to Suggest your Book Amazon Categories

Once you have written a compelling book description and selected your keywords, the next step is to choose the most relevant Amazon categories for your book. Choosing the right categories can help increase your book's visibility and make it easier for potential readers to find your book on Amazon. Here's how you can use ChatGPT to suggest your book Amazon categories:

Step 1: Understand Amazon Categories

Amazon has thousands of categories and subcategories, and it can be overwhelming to choose the most relevant ones for your book. Before you start using ChatGPT, it's essential to understand the Amazon categories and how they work. Amazon categories are a way to classify products and make them easier to find. Books are classified according to genre, subgenre, and topic. Each category has a unique identifier known as a **BISAC (Book Industry Standards and Communications)** code.

Step 2: Generate Category Suggestions with ChatGPT

ChatGPT can help suggest Amazon categories that are most relevant to your book. Here's how to do it:

- Open the ChatGPT website or app and select the text generation tool.

- Write a prompt that describes your book, including its genre, subgenre, and topic.

- Ask ChatGPT to suggest the most relevant Amazon categories for your book.

- Wait for ChatGPT to generate a list of category suggestions.

Step 3: Refine the Category Suggestions

Once ChatGPT has generated a list of category suggestions, you need to refine the list and choose the most relevant categories for your book. Here are some tips to help you refine the category suggestions:

- Read the category descriptions carefully to ensure they accurately describe your book's content.

- Look for categories that have a high level of traffic and low competition.

- Choose categories that are specific to your book's genre and subgenre.

- Use the BISAC codes to find the most accurate categories for your book.

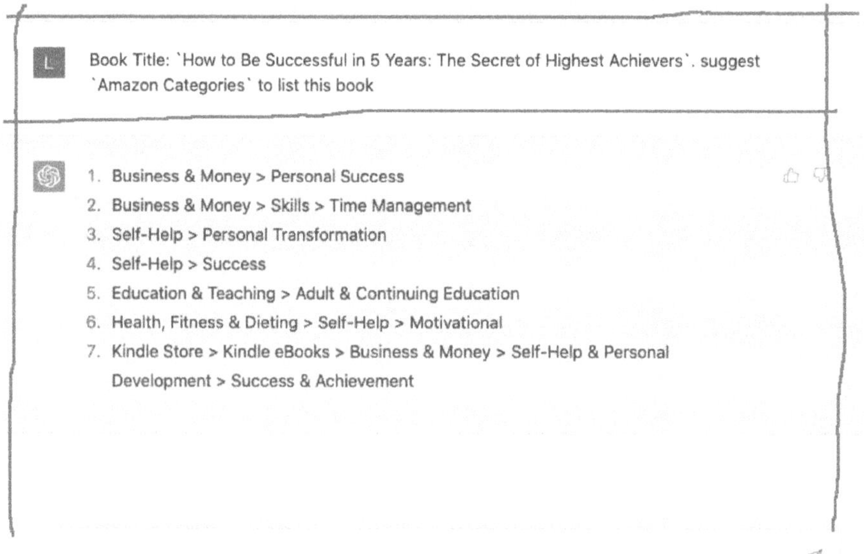

Step 4: Choose the Best Categories for Your Book

Once you have refined the category suggestions, it's time to choose the best categories for your book. Here are some tips to help you choose the best categories:

Choose categories that accurately describe your book's content and are specific to your genre and subgenre.

- Look for categories that have a high level of traffic and low competition.

- Use the BISAC codes to find the most accurate categories for your book.

- Choose categories that are popular and relevant to your target audience.

Step 5: Add Categories to Your Book's Amazon Page

Once you have chosen the best categories for your book, you need to add them to your book's Amazon page. Here's how to do it:

- On your Amazon KDP account and navigate to your book's dashboard.

- Click "Edit Book Details" and on the "Keywords & Categories" tab.

- Enter the BISAC codes for the categories you want to add.

- Save the changes and publish your book.

In conclusion, using ChatGPT to suggest Amazon categories can help increase your book's visibility and make it easier for potential readers to find your book on Amazon. By following these steps and tips, you can use ChatGPT to suggest the most relevant categories for your book and improve your book's chances of success on Amazon.

Chapter 26: Tips and Tricks to Rank your Book in more Categories using the Keywords inputs strategies

Choosing the right Amazon categories and using relevant keywords are crucial to increase your book's visibility on Amazon. However, there are several tips and tricks you can use to improve your book's chances of ranking in more categories using the keyword input strategies. Here are some steps to follow:

Step 1: Use Relevant and Specific Keywords

Using relevant and specific keywords can help your book rank higher in Amazon's search results. When selecting keywords, make sure they accurately describe your book's content and are specific to your genre and subgenre. Avoid using broad or generic keywords as they may not be relevant to your book and will only result in low conversion rates.

Step 2: Use Long-Tail Keywords

Long-tail keywords are more specific and have less competition, making it easier for your book to rank higher in search results. When using long-tail keywords, include descriptive phrases and details about your book's content, such as character names, locations, and themes.

Step 3: Use Relevant Categories

Choosing the most relevant Amazon categories for your book can help improve your book's visibility and increase its chances of ranking higher in more categories. Use ChatGPT to generate category suggestions and refine the list to choose the most accurate and specific categories for your book.

Step 4: Monitor Your Keywords and Categories

Regularly monitor your book's keywords and categories to ensure they are still relevant and accurate. If you notice that your book is not ranking well in certain categories, try adjusting your keywords or adding more specific categories to improve your book's visibility.

Step 5: Optimize Your Book's Amazon Page

Optimizing your book's Amazon page can help improve its chances of ranking higher in search results. Use relevant keywords in your book's title, subtitle, description, and metadata to make it easier for potential readers to find your book.

Step 6: Get More Reviews and Ratings

The number of reviews and ratings your book receives can also impact its visibility and ranking on Amazon. Encourage readers to leave reviews and ratings by offering incentives or creating a community around your book.

Step 7: Promote Your Book

Promoting your book through social media, email marketing, and other channels can help increase its visibility and improve its ranking on Amazon. Use ChatGPT to generate compelling sales pitches, Facebook ads, and video trailers to promote your book and attract more readers.

In conclusion, by following these tips and tricks, you can use keyword input strategies to improve your book's visibility and increase its chances of ranking in more categories on Amazon. Remember to regularly monitor and refine your keywords and categories and optimize your book's Amazon page to attract more potential readers. With ChatGPT's help, you can use data-driven strategies to promote and sell your book on Amazon.

Chapter 27: How to Use ChatGPT to generate your Book Compelling Facebook Ads or Sales Pitch

Creating compelling Facebook ads or sales pitches for your book can help attract more readers and increase your book's visibility on social media. By using ChatGPT, you can generate creative and engaging content for your Facebook ads or sales pitch. Here are some steps to follow:

Step 1: Define Your Target Audience

Before creating Facebook ads or sales pitches, it's important to define your target audience. Use ChatGPT to generate audience profiles, such as age, gender, interests, and location. This will help you create content that resonates with your target audience and drives more engagement.

Step 2: Identify the Key Benefits of Your Book

Identifying the key benefits of your book can help you create compelling Facebook ads or sales pitches that resonate with potential readers. Use ChatGPT to generate key features and benefits of your book and highlight them in your ad or sales pitch.

Step 3: Create Attention-Grabbing Headlines

Creating attention-grabbing headlines can help capture the attention of potential readers and entice them to learn more about your book. Use ChatGPT to generate headline ideas and refine them to create a compelling and attention-grabbing headline.

Step 4: Write a Compelling Description

Writing a compelling description of your book can help convince potential readers to learn more and consider purchasing your book. Use ChatGPT to generate description ideas and refine them to create a compelling and informative description.

Step 5: Add Eye-Catching Images

Adding eye-catching images to your Facebook ad or sales pitch can help attract more attention and improve engagement. Use ChatGPT to generate ideas for images that complement your book and help convey the message of your ad or sales pitch.

Step 6: Include a Call-to-Action

Including a clear call-to-action in your Facebook ad or sales pitch can help encourage potential readers to take action, such as clicking through to your book's Amazon page or signing up for your newsletter. Use ChatGPT to generate ideas for call-to-actions and refine them to create a clear and compelling message.

Step 7: Test and Refine Your Ads

Testing and refining your Facebook ads or sales pitch can help improve their effectiveness and increase engagement. Use ChatGPT to generate ideas for different variations of your ads and test them with your target audience to determine which ones are most effective.

In conclusion, by using ChatGPT to generate compelling content for your Facebook ads or sales pitch, you can attract more readers and increase your book's visibility on social media. Remember to define your target audience, identify the key benefits of your book, create attention-grabbing headlines, write a compelling description, add eye-catching images, include a call-to-action, and test and refine your ads to improve their effectiveness. With ChatGPT's help, you can create data-driven and creative content for your Facebook ads or sales pitch that resonates with your target audience and drives more engagement.

Chapter 28: How to Use ChatGPT to generate Video Trailer Script for your Book Ads

Creating a video trailer for your book can be a powerful way to promote it and reach new readers. With the help of ChatGPT, you can generate a compelling and engaging script for your video trailer. Here are some steps to follow:

Step 1: Define the Message of Your Video Trailer

Before creating a video trailer, it's important to define the message you want to convey. Use ChatGPT to generate ideas for the main message of your video trailer, such as the key benefits of your book or the emotions it evokes.

Step 2: Identify the Key Features and Benefits of Your Book

Identifying the key features and benefits of your book can help you create a video trailer that resonates with potential readers. Use ChatGPT to generate ideas for the key features and benefits of your book, and highlight them in your video trailer script.

Step 3: Create a Compelling Story

Creating a compelling story can help engage viewers and keep them interested in your video trailer. Use ChatGPT to generate ideas for a compelling story, such as the journey of the main character or the challenges they face. Incorporate the key features and benefits of your book into the story to create a compelling and cohesive message.

Step 4: Write an Attention-Grabbing Opening

Writing an attention-grabbing opening can help capture the attention of viewers and entice them to keep watching. Use ChatGPT to generate ideas for an attention-grabbing opening that introduces the main message and sets the tone for the rest of the video.

Step 5: Include Eye-Catching Visuals

Including eye-catching visuals in your video trailer can help keep viewers engaged and convey the message of your book. Use ChatGPT to generate ideas for visuals that complement your story and the key features and benefits of your book.

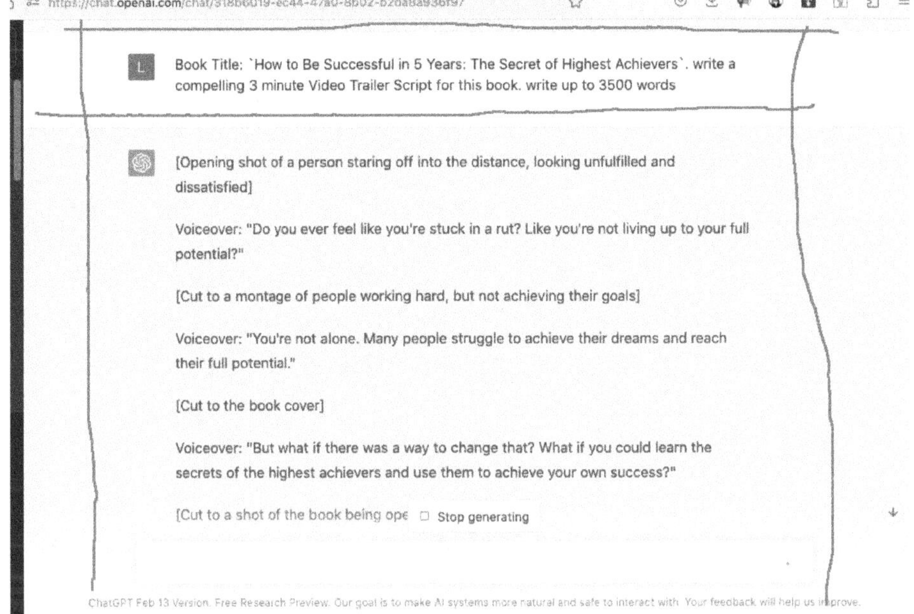

Step 6: Use Engaging Music and Sound Effects

Using engaging music and sound effects in your video trailer can help set the mood and create a memorable viewing experience. Use ChatGPT to generate ideas for music and sound effects that enhance your video trailer and create an emotional connection with viewers.

Step 7: Include a Call-to-Action

Including a clear call-to-action in your video trailer can help encourage viewers to take action, such as visiting your book's Amazon page or signing up for your newsletter. Use ChatGPT to generate ideas for a clear and compelling call-to-action that motivates viewers to take action.

Step 8: Refine and Test Your Script

Refining and testing your video trailer script can help ensure that it effectively conveys the message of your book and resonates with potential readers. Use ChatGPT to generate ideas for different variations of your script and test them with a focus group or on social media to determine which one is most effective.

In conclusion, by using ChatGPT to generate a script for your video trailer, you can create a compelling and engaging message that resonates with potential readers and promotes your book. Remember to define the message of your video trailer, identify the key features and benefits of your book, create a compelling story, write an attention-grabbing opening, include eye-catching visuals, use engaging music and sound effects, include a call-to-action, and refine and test your script to ensure its effectiveness. With ChatGPT's help, you can create a video trailer that effectively promotes your book and attracts more readers.

Chapter 29: How to Use ChatGPT to generate YouTube Video Script for your Book to generate Organic Traffic to your Book

YouTube is an excellent platform to promote your book and generate organic traffic to it. Creating a video about your book is an effective way to attract potential readers and make them interested in your book. However, writing a script for your video can be challenging, especially if you're not used to writing marketing materials. Fortunately, you can use ChatGPT to generate a compelling YouTube video script for your book. In this section, we'll show you how to use ChatGPT to create a script that will engage and persuade your viewers.

Step 1: Define the objective of your video

The first step in creating a YouTube video script is to define the objective of your video. What do you want your viewers to do after watching your video? Do you want them to buy your book, sign up for your newsletter, or visit your website? Defining your objective will help you write a script that is focused and effective.

Step 2: Gather information about your book

To create a compelling script, you need to know the key features of your book, such as the genre, plot, characters, and themes. You can use ChatGPT to gather information about your book by providing it with a summary or blurb. ChatGPT can generate a list of keywords and phrases related to your book, which you can use in your script.

Step 3: Create an outline for your script

Once you have defined your objective and gathered information about your book, it's time to create an outline for your script. The outline should include the key points you want to cover in your video, such as the benefits of reading your book, the plot, and the characters. Use ChatGPT to suggest ideas for your outline and help you organize your thoughts.

Step 4: Write the script

Now it's time to write the script. Use ChatGPT to generate phrases and sentences that you can use in your script. You can start by writing a catchy opening line that will grab your viewers' attention. Then, use ChatGPT to generate descriptions of your book's key features, such as the characters and plot. You can also use ChatGPT to suggest benefits of reading your book, such as entertainment, education, or inspiration.

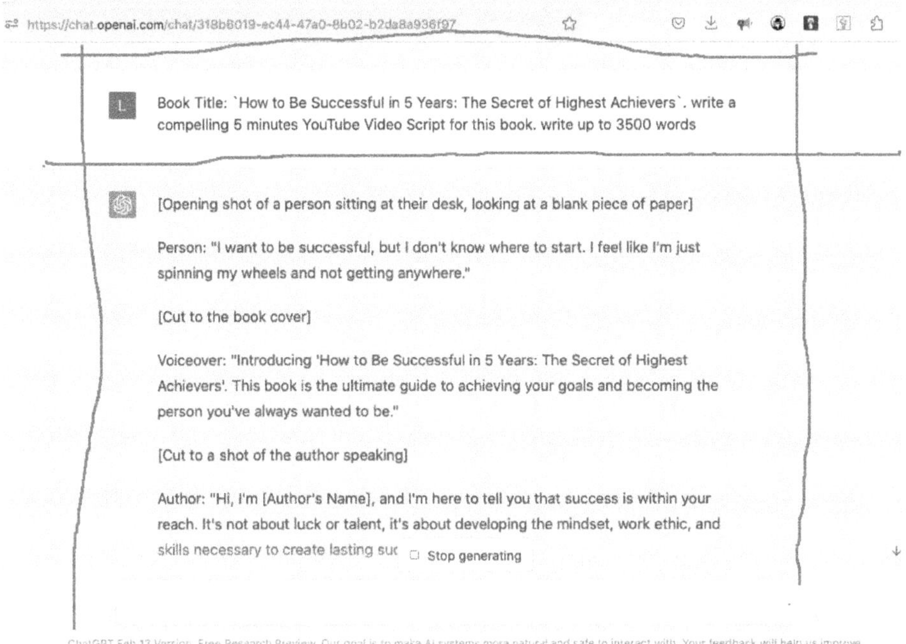

Step 5: Review and edit your script

Once you have written your script, it's important to review and edit it. Make sure that your script is clear, concise, and easy to understand. Check for grammar and spelling errors and make sure that your script is well-structured. You can also use ChatGPT to suggest edits and improvements to your script.

Step 6: Create the video

Once you have a final script, it's time to create the

video. You can use a video editor or **AI Video Creator** to create a professional-looking video. Make sure that your video is visually appealing and engaging. You can use images, graphics, and music to enhance your video.

Step 7: Promote your video

Finally, it's time to promote your video. You can share your video on social media platforms such as Facebook, Twitter, and LinkedIn. You can also embed your video on your website or blog. Make sure to include a call-to-action at the end of your video, such as a link to your book on Amazon or a sign-up form for your newsletter.

In conclusion, using ChatGPT to generate a YouTube video script for your book can help you create a compelling and effective video that will attract potential readers and generate organic traffic to your book. Follow these steps to create a script that will engage and persuade your viewers.

Worksheets

Chapter 30: How to Create a PermaFree ebook on Gumroad and linking it to your Amazon Kindle Account

Creating a permafree ebook on Gumroad and linking it to your Amazon Kindle account is a great way to reach new readers and build your audience. In this guide, we'll walk you through the steps you need to take to make it happen.

Step 1: Sign Up for a Gumroad Account

The first step is to sign up for a Gumroad account if you don't already have one. Gumroad is a platform that allows creators to sell and distribute digital products, including eBooks. To create an account, go to the Gumroad website and click on "Sign Up" in the top right corner. Fill out the form with your information and click "Sign Up" again to create your account.

Step 2: Create Your Ebook

Once you have your Gumroad account set up, it's time to create your ebook. You can do this in any word processing program like Microsoft Word or Google Docs. Make sure to format your document for eBook publication, including setting up the proper margins, page breaks, and font size.

When you're done with your manuscript, you'll need to convert it to a format that Gumroad can use. The two most common formats are EPUB and PDF. You can use a tool like Calibre to convert your manuscript to EPUB format, or save it as a PDF file directly from your word processor.

Step 3: Upload Your Ebook to Gumroad

Once you have your ebook in the proper format, it's time to upload it to Gumroad. To do this, log in to your Gumroad account and click on "Add a Product" in the top right corner. Then, select "Digital Product" from the drop-down menu.

On the next page, you'll be asked to enter information about your ebook, including the title, description, and price. Since we want to set our book as permafree, we'll enter a price of $0.00. You can also add a cover image for your ebook.

Next, you'll need to upload your ebook file. Click on the "Choose File" button and select the EPUB or PDF file you created in the previous step. Then, click "Create Product" to upload your ebook to Gumroad.

Step 4: Set Your Ebook as Permafree

Now that your ebook is uploaded to Gumroad, it's time to set it as permafree. To do this, go to the "Pricing" tab for your product. Under "Pricing Model," select "Pay What You Want." This will allow readers to download your ebook for free, even though the price is listed as $0.00.

Next, under "Minimum Price," enter $0.00. This will ensure that your ebook is always available for free on Gumroad.

Step 5: Request Amazon to Price Match

The final step is to request that Amazon price match your ebook to free. This will make your ebook available for free on the Amazon Kindle store, which is where most readers will be searching for new books.

To request price matching, go to the "Support" tab on your Gumroad product page. Click on "Request Price Match" and enter the ASIN or ISBN of your ebook on Amazon. You'll also need to provide a link to your Gumroad product page.

Amazon typically takes a few days to review price match requests. Once they approve it, your ebook will be available for free on the Kindle store. Note that Amazon may periodically review the price of your book to ensure that it remains free, so be sure to keep an eye on your pricing.

Step 6: Link Your Ebook to Your Kindle Account

Once your ebook is available for free on the Kindle store, it's time to link it to your Kindle account. To do this, go to your Amazon Kindle account and search for your ebook using the title or author name.

Once you have found your ebook, click on the "Buy

now with 1-Click" button. Even though the book is listed as free, Amazon still requires you to "purchase" the book to add it to your Kindle library.

After you've "purchased" the book, it will be added to your Kindle library and you can download it to any of your Kindle devices or apps.

Step 7: Promote Your Permafree Ebook

Now that your permafree ebook is available on both Gumroad and Amazon, it's time to start promoting it to readers. There are several ways you can do this:

1. Share your ebook on social media: Post about your ebook on your social media accounts, including Twitter, Facebook, and Instagram. Be sure to include a link to your Gumroad product page so that readers can download your book for free.

2. Run a promotion: Consider running a promotion on Gumroad to encourage readers to download your ebook. For example, you could offer a limited-time bonus for anyone who downloads your book.

3. Reach out to book bloggers: Look for book bloggers who review eBooks in your genre and reach out to them to ask if they would be interested in reviewing your book.

4. Join author groups: There are many author groups on social media where you can connect with other authors and promote your book.

5. Offer a sample chapter: Consider offering a sample chapter of your ebook for free to give readers a taste of what's inside.

By promoting your permafree ebook, you can reach new readers and build your audience over time.

Conclusion

Creating a permafree ebook on Gumroad and linking it to your Amazon Kindle account is a great way to reach new readers and build your audience. By following the steps in this guide, you can create a permafree ebook and make it available on both Gumroad and Amazon Kindle. Once your ebook is available, be sure to promote it to readers to reach as many people as possible.

Chapter 31: How to Use Smashwords to Create a "PermaFree" Ebook Price Matching With Amazon To Price An Ebook For $0.00 And Ask Amazon To Link The Ebook To My Kindle Account

Smashwords is another platform that allows you to publish and distribute your ebooks. In this guide, we will walk you through the process of creating a "permafree" ebook on Smashwords and linking it to your Kindle account on Amazon.

Step 1: Create an Account on Smashwords

The first step in creating a "permafree" ebook on Smashwords is to create an account on the platform. To do this, go to the Smashwords homepage and click on "Join" at the top of the page. Follow the prompts to create your account and set up your author profile.

Step 2: Upload Your Ebook

Once your account is set up, you can upload your ebook to Smashwords. To do this, click on "Publish" at the top of the page and select "Ebook." Then, follow the prompts to upload your ebook file and fill out the necessary information, including the title, author name, and book description.

Step 3: Set Your Price to $0.00

To make your ebook "permafree," you need to set the price to $0.00 on Smashwords. To do this, go to the "Publishing" section of your ebook's page and click on "Pricing." Then, select "Free" and save your changes.

Step 4: Distribute Your Ebook

Once your ebook is uploaded and set to "permafree," you can distribute it to other ebook retailers, including Amazon Kindle. To do this, go to the "Publishing" section of your ebook's page and click on "Distribution." Then, select "Amazon" and follow the prompts to set up your distribution.

Step 5: Link Your Ebook to Your Kindle Account

After your ebook is distributed to Amazon Kindle, you need to link it to your Kindle account. To do this, go to your Amazon Kindle dashboard and click on "Books" at the top of the page. Then, select "Add a New Title" and follow the prompts to add your ebook.

During the upload process, you will be asked to enter the book's title, author name, and other information. Be sure to enter the same information that you used when uploading your ebook to Smashwords. This will ensure that your ebook is linked correctly.

Step 6: Verify Your Ebook is "Permafree" on Amazon

After your ebook is uploaded to Amazon, it's

important to verify that it is set to "permafree." To do this, go to your book's page on Amazon and check the price. It should be listed as $0.00.

Step 7: Promote Your Ebook

Once your ebook is set to "permafree" on Amazon, it's time to promote it to readers. Here are a few ways you can do this:

1. **Use social media:** Share your ebook on social media, including Twitter, Facebook, and Instagram. Be sure to include a link to your book's Amazon page so that readers can download it for free.

2. **Reach out to book bloggers:** Look for book bloggers who review eBooks in your genre and reach out to them to ask if they would be interested in reviewing your book.

3. **Run ads:** Consider running ads on social media or Amazon to promote your book to a wider audience.

4. **Join author groups:** There are many author groups on social media where you can connect with other authors and promote your book to their readers.

Conclusion

By following the steps in this guide, you can upload your ebook to Smashwords, set the price to $0.00, distribute it to Amazon Kindle, and link it to your Kindle account. This will allow readers to download your ebook for free and help you reach a wider audience.

Remember, promoting your ebook is just as important as publishing it. By using social media, book bloggers, and ads, you can attract new readers and build a following for your work. Keep in mind that it may take time to see results, but with persistence and dedication, you can achieve your goals.

We hope this guide has been helpful in showing you how to use Smashwords to create a "permafree" ebook and link it to your Kindle account on Amazon. Good luck with your ebook publishing journey!

Chapter 32: How to Use BookFunnel to Create a "PermaFree" Ebook Price Matching With Amazon To Price An Ebook For $0.00 And Ask Amazon To Link The Ebook To My Kindle Account

BookFunnel is a popular platform that helps authors distribute and sell their ebooks directly to readers. In addition to selling ebooks, BookFunnel also allows you to create a "permafree" ebook, which means you can distribute your ebook for free indefinitely. In this guide, we'll show you how to use BookFunnel to create a "permafree" ebook, set the price to $0.00, distribute it to Amazon Kindle, and link it to your Kindle account.

Step 1: Create an Account on BookFunnel

To get started, you'll need to create an account on BookFunnel. Simply go to the BookFunnel website and click on the "Get Started" button. Follow the prompts to set up your account and create a new book.

Step 2: Upload Your Ebook

Once you've created your account, you can upload your ebook to BookFunnel. To do this, click on the "Add New Book" button and select the file from your computer. BookFunnel supports a wide range of ebook formats, including EPUB, MOBI, and PDF.

Step 3: Set Your Ebook Price to $0.00

After uploading your ebook, you'll need to set the price to $0.00 to make it free. To do this, go to the "Pricing" section of your book settings and select "Free" as the price.

Step 4: Distribute Your Ebook to Amazon Kindle

Once your ebook is uploaded and priced at $0.00, you can distribute it to Amazon Kindle. BookFunnel offers two ways to distribute your ebook to Kindle:

- Option 1: Use BookFunnel to distribute your ebook directly to readers' Kindle devices. To do this, you'll need to enable the "Send to Kindle" feature in your book settings. Readers can then download your ebook directly to their Kindle devices by clicking on the "Send to Kindle" button.

- Option 2: Use BookFunnel to generate a download link that readers can use to download your ebook from Amazon. To do this, go to the "Distribution" section of your book settings and select "Amazon" as the retailer. BookFunnel will generate a download link that you can share with readers.

Step 5: Link Your Ebook to Your Kindle

Account

Once your ebook is available on Amazon, you can link it to your Kindle account so that you can download and read it on your own Kindle device or app.

To do this, follow these steps:

- Go to the Amazon website and sign in to your account.
- Click on the "Account & Lists" button in the top-right corner of the screen.
- Click on the "Content and Devices" button.
- Select the "Preferences" tab.
- Scroll down to the "Personal Document Settings" section and click on the "Add a new approved e-mail address" button.
- Enter the email address associated with your BookFunnel account and click on the "Add Address" button.
- BookFunnel will now be an approved email address for your Kindle account.
- Go back to BookFunnel and find the download link for your ebook on Amazon.
- Click on the download link and select "Send to Kindle" from the dropdown menu.
- Choose your preferred device or app from the list and click on the "Send" button.

Your ebook will now be sent to your Kindle device or app, and you'll be able to download and read it just like any other Kindle book.

Conclusion

BookFunnel is a user-friendly platform that allows authors to easily distribute their ebooks to readers. By creating a "permafree" ebook on BookFunnel, you can distribute your book for free indefinitely, making it accessible to a wider audience. Additionally, BookFunnel's integration with Amazon Kindle makes it easy to distribute your ebook to Kindle users and link it to your own Kindle account. By following the steps outlined in this guide, you can create a "permafree" ebook on BookFunnel, set the price to $0.00, and distribute it to Amazon Kindle, giving your book maximum exposure and helping you reach more readers.

Chapter 33: How to Use Instafreebie to Create a "PermaFree" Ebook Price Matching With Amazon To Price An Ebook For $0.00 And Ask Amazon To Link The Ebook To My Kindle Account

Instafreebie was a popular platform for distributing free ebooks, but it has since been rebranded as Prolific Works. In this guide, we will outline the steps to use Prolific Works to create a "permafree" ebook, set the price to $0.00, and distribute it to Amazon Kindle, making it accessible to a wider audience.

Step 1: Create a Prolific Works Account

To get started, go to the Prolific Works website and create an account. You can sign up for free and choose a plan that works best for you, depending on the number of books you want to distribute and the features you need.

Step 2: Create Your Ebook

Before you can distribute your ebook on Prolific Works, you need to create it in a compatible format. Prolific Works accepts EPUB, MOBI, and PDF formats. If you have your ebook in a different format, you can use an ebook conversion tool such as Calibre to convert it to the required format.

Step 3: Upload Your Ebook to Prolific Works

Once you have your ebook in the right format, log in to your Prolific Works account and navigate to the "Dashboard" page. Click on "Create a New Book" and follow the prompts to upload your ebook file, add a book cover, and enter other relevant information such as the book's title, author name, and description.

Step 4: Set the Price to $0.00

After you have uploaded your ebook, go to the "Pricing" section and set the price to $0.00. This will make your book available for free to readers who download it from Prolific Works.

Step 5: Distribute Your Ebook to Amazon Kindle

To distribute your ebook to Amazon Kindle, go to the "Distribution" section and click on "Add Retailer." Select "Amazon Kindle" from the list of retailers and enter your Amazon KDP account information. This will link your Prolific Works account to your Amazon Kindle account and enable you to distribute your ebook to Kindle readers.

Step 6: Link Your Ebook to Your Kindle Account

To link your ebook to your Kindle account, you need to

provide Amazon with the ASIN (Amazon Standard Identification Number) for your ebook. You can find the ASIN in the "Product Information" section of your ebook's listing on Amazon. Copy the ASIN and go back to Prolific Works. In the "Distribution" section, click on "Link Your Amazon Account" and paste the ASIN in the appropriate field. Click on "Link Account" to complete the process.

Step 7: Promote Your Ebook

Now that your ebook is available for free on Prolific Works and linked to your Amazon Kindle account, it's time to promote it. You can use social media, email marketing, and other channels to promote your book and reach more readers. You can also use Prolific Works' built-in marketing tools to promote your book to its audience of avid readers.

Conclusion: Prolific Works is a powerful platform for distributing free ebooks and reaching a wider audience of readers. By creating a "permafree" ebook on Prolific Works, you can distribute your book for free indefinitely, making it accessible to a wider audience.

Additionally, Prolific Works' integration with Amazon Kindle makes it easy to distribute your ebook to Kindle users and link it to your own Kindle account. By following the steps outlined in this guide, you can create a "permafree" ebook on Prolific Works, set the price to $0.00, and distribute it to Amazon Kindle, giving your book maximum exposure and helping you reach more readers.

Chapter 34: How to link and sell your same books on Amazon KDP and `Barnes & Noble Press`

Here are the step-by-step instructions:

1. **Prepare Your Book Files:** Before you start publishing your book on both Amazon KDP and Barnes & Noble Press, you need to ensure that your book files are ready. You will need the following files:
   - eBook files: EPUB or MOBI format for Barnes & Noble Press, and MOBI or PDF format for Amazon KDP.
   - Paperback files: PDF file for both Amazon KDP and Barnes & Noble Press.
2. **Create an Amazon KDP Account:** If you don't already have an Amazon KDP account, you need to create one. To do this, go to kdp.amazon.com and click on "Sign up". Follow the prompts to create your account. You will need to provide your personal information, including your name, address, and bank account details.

3. **Upload Your Book to Amazon KDP:** Once you have created your account, you can upload your book to Amazon KDP. Click on "Create a

New Title" and follow the prompts to enter your book details, upload your book file, and set your price.

4. **Create a Barnes & Noble Press Account:** To sell your book on Barnes & Noble Press, you need to create an account. Go to press.barnesandnoble.com and click on "Sign up". Follow the prompts to create your account. You will need to provide your personal information, including your name, address, and bank account details.

5. **Upload Your Book to Barnes & Noble Press:** Once you have created your account, you can upload your book to Barnes & Noble Press. Click on "Add a Title" and follow the prompts to enter your book details, upload your book file, and set your price.

6. **Link Your Book Listings:** To link your book listings on Amazon KDP and Barnes & Noble Press, you need to include the same book information and ISBN for both platforms. Here are the steps to follow:

   - Go to your Amazon KDP account and find your book listing. Copy the ISBN number.
   - Go to your Barnes & Noble Press account and find your book listing. Paste the ISBN

number into the ISBN field.
- Make sure that the book title, author name, and book description are the same on both platforms.
- Save the changes to your book listing on Barnes & Noble Press.

7. **Sell Your Book:** Now that your book is listed on both Amazon KDP and Barnes & Noble Press, you can start selling it. You can promote your book on both platforms, and readers can purchase it from either platform.

8. **Manage Your Sales and Royalties:** You can manage your sales and royalties on both Amazon KDP and Barnes & Noble Press. Amazon KDP provides sales reports and pays royalties monthly, while Barnes & Noble Press provides sales reports and pays royalties quarterly.

Conclusion: By following these steps, you can link and sell your books on Amazon KDP and Barnes & Noble Press. It's important to ensure that your book files are properly formatted and that your book information is consistent across both platforms. With these two powerful sales channels at your disposal, you can reach a wider audience and sell more copies of your book.

Chapter 35: How to link and sell your same books on Amazon KDP and `Kobo Writing Life`

Here are the step-by-step instructions:

1. **Prepare Your Book Files:** Before you start publishing your book on both Amazon KDP and Kobo Writing Life, you need to ensure that your book files are ready. You will need the following files:
   - eBook files: EPUB format for Kobo Writing Life, and MOBI or PDF format for Amazon KDP.
   - Paperback files: PDF file for both Amazon KDP and Kobo Writing Life.

2. **Create an Amazon KDP Account:** If you don't already have an Amazon KDP account, you need to create one. To do this, go to kdp.amazon.com and click on "Sign up". Follow the prompts to create your account. You will need to provide your personal information, including your name, address, and bank account details.

3. **Upload Your Book to Amazon KDP:** Once you have created your account, you can upload your book to Amazon KDP. Click on "Create a New Title" and follow the prompts to enter your

book details, upload your book file, and set your price.

4. **Create a Kobo Writing Life Account:** To sell your book on Kobo Writing Life, you need to create an account. Go to writinglife.kobobooks.com and click on "Sign up". Follow the prompts to create your account. You will need to provide your personal information, including your name, address, and bank account details.

5. **Upload Your Book to Kobo Writing Life:** Once you have created your account, you can upload your book to Kobo Writing Life. Click on "Add eBook" and follow the prompts to enter your book details, upload your book file, and set your price.

6. **Link Your Book Listings:** To link your book listings on Amazon KDP and Kobo Writing Life, you need to include the same book information and ISBN for both platforms. Here are the steps to follow:

   - Go to your Amazon KDP account and find your book listing. Copy the ISBN number.
   - Go to your Kobo Writing Life account and find your book listing. Paste the ISBN number into the ISBN field.
   - Make sure that the book title, author

name, and book description are the same on both platforms.

- Save the changes to your book listing on Kobo Writing Life.

7. **Sell Your Book:** Now that your book is listed on both Amazon KDP and Kobo Writing Life, you can start selling it. You can promote your book on both platforms, and readers can purchase it from either platform.

8. **Manage Your Sales and Royalties:** You can manage your sales and royalties on both Amazon KDP and Kobo Writing Life. Amazon KDP provides sales reports and pays royalties monthly, while Kobo Writing Life provides sales reports and pays royalties quarterly.

Conclusion: By following these steps, you can link and sell your books on Amazon KDP and Kobo Writing Life. It's important to ensure that your book files are properly formatted and that your book information is consistent across both platforms. With these two powerful sales channels at your disposal, you can reach a wider audience and sell more copies of your book.

Chapter 36: How to link and sell your same books on Amazon KDP and `Apple Books`

Here are the step-by-step instructions:

1. **Prepare Your Book Files:** Before you start publishing your book on both Amazon KDP and Apple Books, you need to ensure that your book files are ready. You will need the following files:
    - eBook files: EPUB format for Apple Books, and MOBI or PDF format for Amazon KDP.
    - Paperback files: PDF file for Amazon KDP.
2. **Create an Amazon KDP Account:** If you don't already have an Amazon KDP account, you need to create one. To do this, go to kdp.amazon.com and click on "Sign up". Follow the prompts to create your account. You will need to provide your personal information, including your name, address, and bank account details.

3. **Upload Your Book to Amazon KDP:** Once you have created your account, you can upload your book to Amazon KDP. Click on "Create a New Title" and follow the prompts to enter your book details, upload your book file, and set your price.

4. **Create an Apple Books Account:** To sell your book on Apple Books, you need to create an account. Go to iTunes Connect (itunesconnect.apple.com) and sign in with your Apple ID. Click on "Agreements, Tax, and Banking" and follow the prompts to set up your banking information and tax information.

5. **Add Your Book to iTunes Connect:** Once you have set up your account, you can add your book to iTunes Connect. Click on "My Books" and then click on the "+" icon to add a new book. Follow the prompts to enter your book details, upload your book file, and set your price.

6. **Link Your Book Listings:** To link your book listings on Amazon KDP and Apple Books, you need to include the same book information and ISBN for both platforms. Here are the steps to follow:

    -   Go to your Amazon KDP account and find your book listing. Copy the ISBN number.
    -   Go to your Apple Books account and find your book listing. Paste the ISBN number into the "ISBN" field.
    -   Make sure that the book title, author name, and book description are the same on both platforms.
    -   Save the changes to your book listing on

Apple Books.

7. **Sell Your Book:** Now that your book is listed on both Amazon KDP and Apple Books, you can start selling it. You can promote your book on both platforms, and readers can purchase it from either platform.

8. **Manage Your Sales and Royalties:** You can manage your sales and royalties on both Amazon KDP and Apple Books. Amazon KDP provides sales reports and pays royalties monthly, while Apple Books provides sales reports and pays royalties quarterly.

Conclusion: By following these steps, you can link and sell your books on Amazon KDP and Apple Books. It's important to ensure that your book files are properly formatted and that your book information is consistent across both platforms. With these two powerful sales channels at your disposal, you can reach a wider audience and sell more copies of your book.

Chapter 37: How to link and sell your same books on Amazon KDP and `Google Play Books`

Here are the step-by-step instructions:

1. **Prepare Your Book Files:** Before you start publishing your book on both Amazon KDP and Google Play Books, you need to ensure that your book files are ready. You will need the following files:
   - eBook files: EPUB format for Google Play Books, and MOBI or PDF format for Amazon KDP.
   - Paperback files: PDF file for Amazon KDP.
2. **Create an Amazon KDP Account:** If you don't already have an Amazon KDP account, you need to create one. To do this, go to kdp.amazon.com and click on "Sign up". Follow the prompts to create your account. You will need to provide your personal information, including your name, address, and bank account details.

3. **Upload Your Book to Amazon KDP:** Once you have created your account, you can upload your book to Amazon KDP. Click on "Create a New Title" and follow the prompts to enter your book details, upload your book file, and set your

price.

4. **Create a Google Play Books Account:** To sell your book on Google Play Books, you need to create a Google Play Books Partner account. Go to play.google.com/books/publish and sign in with your Google account. Follow the prompts to set up your account, provide your banking information, and accept the terms and conditions.

5. **Add Your Book to Google Play Books:** Once you have set up your account, you can add your book to Google Play Books. Click on "Add a Book" and follow the prompts to enter your book details, upload your book file, and set your price.

6. **Link Your Book Listings:** To link your book listings on Amazon KDP and Google Play Books, you need to include the same book information and ISBN for both platforms. Here are the steps to follow:

    - Go to your Amazon KDP account and find your book listing. Copy the ISBN number.
    - Go to your Google Play Books account and find your book listing. Paste the ISBN number into the "ISBN" field.
    - Make sure that the book title, author name, and book description are the same on both platforms.

- Save the changes to your book listing on Google Play Books.
-

7. **Sell Your Book:** Now that your book is listed on both Amazon KDP and Google Play Books, you can start selling it. You can promote your book on both platforms, and readers can purchase it from either platform.

8. **Manage Your Sales and Royalties:** You can manage your sales and royalties on both Amazon KDP and Google Play Books. Amazon KDP provides sales reports and pays royalties monthly, while Google Play Books provides sales reports and pays royalties monthly as well.

Conclusion: By following these steps, you can link and sell your books on Amazon KDP and Google Play Books. It's important to ensure that your book files are properly formatted and that your book information is consistent across both platforms. With these two powerful sales channels at your disposal, you can reach a wider audience and sell more copies of your book.

Chapter 38: How to link and sell your same books on Amazon KDP and `Smashwords`

Here are the step-by-step instructions:

1. **Prepare Your Book Files:** Before you start publishing your book on both Amazon KDP and Smashwords, you need to ensure that your book files are ready. You will need the following files:
    - eBook files: EPUB format for Smashwords, and MOBI or PDF format for Amazon KDP.
    - Paperback files: PDF file for Amazon KDP.
2. **Create an Amazon KDP Account:** If you don't already have an Amazon KDP account, you need to create one. To do this, go to kdp.amazon.com and click on "Sign up". Follow the prompts to create your account. You will need to provide your personal information, including your name, address, and bank account details.

3. **Upload Your Book to Amazon KDP:** Once you have created your account, you can upload your book to Amazon KDP. Click on "Create a New Title" and follow the prompts to enter your book details, upload your book file, and set your price.

4. **Create a Smashwords Account:** To sell your book on Smashwords, you need to create a Smashwords account. Go to smashwords.com and click on "Sign up". Follow the prompts to set up your account, provide your banking information, and accept the terms and conditions.

5. **Add Your Book to Smashwords:** Once you have set up your account, you can add your book to Smashwords. Click on "Publish" and follow the prompts to enter your book details, upload your book file, and set your price.

6. **Link Your Book Listings:** To link your book listings on Amazon KDP and Smashwords, you need to include the same book information and ISBN for both platforms. Here are the steps to follow:

   - Go to your Amazon KDP account and find your book listing. Copy the ISBN number.
   - Go to your Smashwords account and find your book listing. Paste the ISBN number into the "ISBN" field.
   - Make sure that the book title, author name, and book description are the same on both platforms.
   - Save the changes to your book listing on Smashwords.

7. **Sell Your Book:** Now that your book is listed on both Amazon KDP and Smashwords, you can start selling it. You can promote your book on both platforms, and readers can purchase it from either platform.

8. **Manage Your Sales and Royalties:** You can manage your sales and royalties on both Amazon KDP and Smashwords. Amazon KDP provides sales reports and pays royalties monthly, while Smashwords provides sales reports and pays royalties quarterly.

Conclusion: By following these steps, you can link and sell your books on Amazon KDP and Smashwords. It's important to ensure that your book files are properly formatted and that your book information is consistent across both platforms. With these two powerful sales channels at your disposal, you can reach a wider audience and sell more copies of your book.

Chapter 39: How to link and sell your same books on Amazon KDP and `Draft2Digital`

Here are the step-by-step instructions:

1. **Prepare Your Book Files:** Before you start publishing your book on both Amazon KDP and Draft2Digital, you need to ensure that your book files are ready. You will need the following files:
    - eBook files: EPUB format for Draft2Digital, and MOBI or PDF format for Amazon KDP.
    - Paperback files: PDF file for Amazon KDP.
2. **Create an Amazon KDP Account:** If you don't already have an Amazon KDP account, you need to create one. To do this, go to kdp.amazon.com and click on "Sign up". Follow the prompts to create your account. You will need to provide your personal information, including your name, address, and bank account details.

3. **Upload Your Book to Amazon KDP:** Once you have created your account, you can upload your book to Amazon KDP. Click on "Create a New Title" and follow the prompts to enter your book details, upload your book file, and set your

price.

4. **Create a Draft2Digital Account:** To sell your book on Draft2Digital, you need to create a Draft2Digital account. Go to draft2digital.com and click on "Sign up". Follow the prompts to set up your account, provide your banking information, and accept the terms and conditions.

5. **Add Your Book to Draft2Digital:** Once you have set up your account, you can add your book to Draft2Digital. Click on "Add New Book" and follow the prompts to enter your book details, upload your book file, and set your price.

6. **Link Your Book Listings:** To link your book listings on Amazon KDP and Draft2Digital, you need to include the same book information and ISBN for both platforms. Here are the steps to follow:

    - Go to your Amazon KDP account and find your book listing. Copy the ISBN number.
    - Go to your Draft2Digital account and find your book listing. Paste the ISBN number into the "ISBN" field.
    - Make sure that the book title, author name, and book description are the same on both platforms.
    - Save the changes to your book listing on

Draft2Digital.

7. **Sell Your Book:** Now that your book is listed on both Amazon KDP and Draft2Digital, you can start selling it. You can promote your book on both platforms, and readers can purchase it from either platform.

8. **Manage Your Sales and Royalties:** You can manage your sales and royalties on both Amazon KDP and Draft2Digital. Amazon KDP provides sales reports and pays royalties monthly, while Draft2Digital provides sales reports and pays royalties quarterly.

Conclusion: By following these steps, you can link and sell your books on Amazon KDP and Draft2Digital. It's important to ensure that your book files are properly formatted and that your book information is consistent across both platforms. With these two powerful sales channels at your disposal, you can reach a wider audience and sell more copies of your book.

Chapter 40: How to link and sell your same books on Amazon KDP and `BookBaby`

Here are the step-by-step instructions:

1. **Prepare Your Book Files:** Before you start publishing your book on both Amazon KDP and BookBaby, you need to ensure that your book files are ready. You will need the following files:
   - eBook files: EPUB format for BookBaby and MOBI or PDF format for Amazon KDP.
   - Paperback files: PDF file for Amazon KDP.
2. **Create an Amazon KDP Account:** If you don't already have an Amazon KDP account, you need to create one. To do this, go to kdp.amazon.com and click on "Sign up". Follow the prompts to create your account. You will need to provide your personal information, including your name, address, and bank account details.

3. **Upload Your Book to Amazon KDP:** Once you have created your account, you can upload your book to Amazon KDP. Click on "Create a New Title" and follow the prompts to enter your

book details, upload your book file, and set your price.

4. **Create a BookBaby Account:** To sell your book on BookBaby, you need to create a BookBaby account. Go to bookbaby.com and click on "Sign up". Follow the prompts to set up your account, provide your banking information, and accept the terms and conditions.

5. **Add Your Book to BookBaby:** Once you have set up your account, you can add your book to BookBaby. Click on "Add New Title" and follow the prompts to enter your book details, upload your book file, and set your price.

6. **Link Your Book Listings:** To link your book listings on Amazon KDP and BookBaby, you need to include the same book information and ISBN for both platforms. Here are the steps to follow:

   - Go to your Amazon KDP account and find your book listing. Copy the ISBN number.
   - Go to your BookBaby account and find your book listing. Paste the ISBN number into the "ISBN" field.
   - Make sure that the book title, author name, and book description are the same on both platforms.
   - Save the changes to your book listing on

BookBaby.

7. **Sell Your Book:** Now that your book is listed
    on both Amazon KDP and BookBaby, you can
    start selling it. You can promote your book on
    both platforms, and readers can purchase it
    from either platform.

8. **Manage Your Sales and Royalties:** You can
    manage your sales and royalties on both Amazon
    KDP and BookBaby. Amazon KDP provides sales
    reports and pays royalties monthly, while
    BookBaby provides sales reports and pays
    royalties quarterly.

Conclusion: By following these steps, you can link and
sell your books on Amazon KDP and BookBaby. It's
important to ensure that your book files are properly
formatted and that your book information is
consistent across both platforms. With these two
powerful sales channels at your disposal, you can
reach a wider audience and sell more copies of your
book.

If you Buy/Download my Book and found it interesting, I will be glad; if you can leave a nice Review for this book, this will help other potential readers to show interest.

It will take only 30 seconds and it will be greatly appreciated.

Click Here to Leave a Review!

Thank you in advance, I love you and you are the best.

Conclusion

Congratulations on reaching the end of this comprehensive guide on the *The Psychology of Kindle Sales: How to Sell your eBooks on Amazon KDP!* We hope that the insights and strategies presented here will help you achieve your goal of selling your first 1000 copies, getting reviews without breaking a sweat, and earning $1000 to $20,000 per month.

Throughout this book, we have emphasized the importance of creating high-quality, engaging content that meets the needs and desires of your target audience. We have discussed various strategies for promoting your book on Amazon and other platforms, including social media, YouTube, and email marketing.

We have also introduced you to the power of ChatGPT, a cutting-edge artificial intelligence tool that can help you speed up your book upload and promotion process. With ChatGPT, you can generate compelling book cover designs, Amazon descriptions, keywords, categories, Facebook ads, and video trailer scripts in a matter of minutes.

However, it's important to remember that there is no magic bullet when it comes to selling books on Amazon. It takes hard work, dedication, and persistence to achieve success in this competitive marketplace.

Here are some key takeaways from this book that can help you succeed:

1. Create high-quality, engaging content that meets the needs and desires of your target audience.

2. Invest in professional editing, formatting, and cover design to make your book stand out from the crowd.

3. Use effective marketing strategies to promote your book, including social media, YouTube, email marketing, and paid advertising.

4. Build an email list and engage with your readers regularly to build a loyal fan base.

5. Use ChatGPT to speed up your book upload and promotion process, but don't rely on it entirely.

6. Continuously monitor your book's performance and adjust your marketing strategies as needed.

7. Stay up to date with the latest trends and best practices in book publishing and marketing.

Remember, success on Amazon Kindle is not a one-time event. It's an ongoing process that requires constant effort and attention. But with the right mindset, skills, and tools, you can achieve your goals and build a successful career as a Kindle author.

We wish you the best of luck in your journey and hope that you will use the knowledge and insights presented in this book to achieve your full potential as an author.

Thank you for reading!

Book Recommendations
Think of Picking your Next Book! My Recommendations:
Thanks! You are Blessed as you Bless me!

The Art of Storytelling: ChatGPT's Guide to Writing Compelling Fiction

GumRoad Mastery Self-Publishing: Boosting Sales and Building Audience for Your Book Ultimate Guide

Book Recommendations

Think of Picking your Next Book! My Recommendations:
Thanks! You are Blessed as you Bless me!

ChatGPT Secret Weapon: 5 Steps to Start Writing and Selling Books within 24 Hours

The Future of Writing and Selling Books: A Guide to ChatGPT-3 AI Technology

Book Recommendations

ChatGPT + YouTube Channel or Real Estate: How to Make $10,000-$50,000 Monthly

Still Dismissing TikTok as Something for the kids? : Short-form video content created by ChatGPT is exploding right now!

Book Recommendations

REPEAT AFTER ME; I AM A MILLIONAIRE: THE SECRET OF THE MILLIONAIRES

The 4 Pillars of Wealth Creation

Book Recommendations

The Mindset of Financial Planning: Make it, Manage it, and Invest it - the Beginner Guide to Financial Freedom

Get Started with Pictory AI Video Creation: The Beginner Cookbook

Book Recommendations

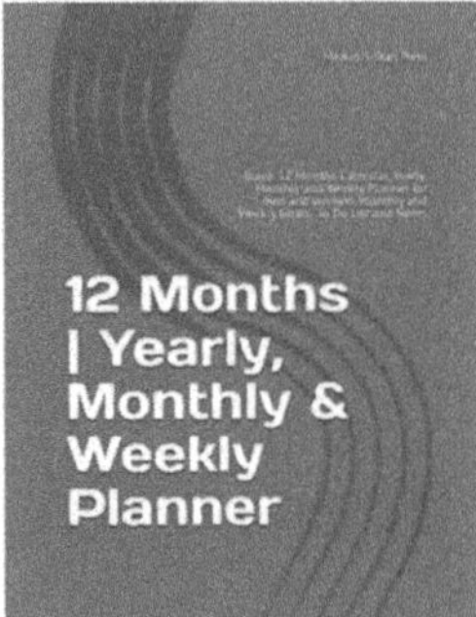

12 Months | Yearly, Monthly & Weekly Planner: Blank 12 Months Calendar, Yearly, Monthly, and Weekly Planner Paperback

ChatGPT with Fiverr and Upwork: 30 Freelancing Job you can Start Immediately using ChatGPT to Generate Ideas and Content for your Clients